COUNSEL TO CHRISTIANS

BY

GEORGE MÜLLER

FOURTH EDITION

The Content of George Müller's work is in the Public Domain.

Book cover and Foreword © by Eternally Blessed 2013.
All rights reserved.

CONTENTS

FOREWORD
(page vii)
PREFACE
TO THE FIRST EDITION (page xiii)
CHAPTER I
COUNSELS TO CONVERTS

Reading the Scriptures — Conviction of sin — Trust in Christ — Uprightness — Denying ungodliness — Fruitfulness — Living Christ — Confession and forgiveness — Confessing Christ — Growth in Christ — Old enemies — Church fellowship. (page 15)

CHAPTER II
COUNSELS TO CONVERTS (continued)

The manner of reading the Word — Stick to the Word of God — Consecutive reading — The connection of Scripture — Benefit of consecutive reading — A special benefit — Reading the Word prayerfully — An illustration of this — Meditate on the Word — Make the meditation personal — Read in faith—Be doers of the Word—The fulness of the revelation given in the Word — Prayer — Faith must come first — Courage — Knowledge — Temperance — Patience — Godliness. (page 29)

CHAPTER III
COUNSELS TO CONVERTS (continued)

A substitute — Points already considered — Brotherly

kindness — Charity — The result of this, Fruit — The contrary result — Make our calling and election sure — Not a stony-ground hearer — Diligence — An abundant entrance — True strength — Put on the whole armour of God — Stand against the wiles of the Devil. (page 45)

CHAPTER IV
COUNSELS TO CONVERTS (continued)

We must put on the whole armour of God — The Captain of our salvation — "Wherefore take unto you" — "Be of good courage" — That old serpent which is the devil — "Evil day" — The sleep of death — "And having done all to stand" — "Having your loins girt about with truth" — The breastplate of righteousness — The righteousness of Christ — "The preparation of the gospel of peace" — "Above all, taking the shield of faith" — "Fiery darts" — Temporal trials — An illustration — "And take the helmet of salvation" — The sword of the Spirit — Praying and watching. (page 59)

CHAPTER V
COUNSELS TO CONVERTS (continued)

Marking answers to prayer — Reviewing answered prayers — The effects of thus reviewing answered prayers — Freedom from anxiety — We have, however, such a Friend — Lean upon Him alone — The folly of neglecting this injunction — "Supplication" — "Thanksgiving" — The certain effect of all this — "Keep your hearts." (page 77)

CHAPTER VI
COUNSELS TO CONVERTS (continued)

The consequences of sin — Self-abasement — "Jehovah is my portion" — "Is God Himself my portion?" — Hoping and waiting — The conclusion of the matter. (page 85)

CHAPTER VII
THE GOD OF JESHURUN

Imputed righteousness — Saved by grace through faith — Oh, glorious gospel! — The Lord our portion — The Lord our strength — The Lord our deliverer — Trying circumstances — The eternal God is our refuge — "The eternal God" — "False views of Christianity" — What does God want? — "The living God is thy refuge" — The Deliverer — Jehovah saves — God's deliverances — "Israel then shall dwell in safety alone" — Separate from the world — We ought to be a "marked people" — Fruitfulness — "Happy art thou, O Israel" — Never attempt to carry your own burden — Cause for happiness. (page 97)

CHAPTER VIII
THE SECRET OF PREVAILING PRAYER

Satan's power limited — "Prayer without ceasing" — "Waiting for an answer — God's manner of answering the prayer — The unchangeable power of God — The deliverance effected —Failing faith—If we ask, let us he looking for the answer. (page 113)

CHAPTER IX
THE BRIDE OF CHRIST

The character of the Book — The names given to the church — The absent Bridegroom — Do we belong to the spouse of Christ or not? — "A garden enclosed" — The believer is not his own — "A spring shut up" — "A fountain sealed" — Joy of Christ in His church — An illustration — Accepted service — Bearing the infirmities of the weak — Christ's estimate of His bride — "A fountain of gardens" — "A well of living waters" —

"Streams from Lebanon" — Strong in the armour of God — Reciprocal delight — Gratify the heart of Jesus — The Lord's response — The invitation. (page 123)

CHAPTER X

THE POWER OF THE KING

One with the King — Power in the King in our weakness — Reverence — Power — Righteousness — Judgment — The certainty of Christ's triumph. (page 139)

CHAPTER XI

THE KNOWLEDGE OF CHRIST

Practical results of knowing Christ — How to attain the knowledge of Christ. (Page 149)

CHAPTER XII

TRANSFORMED IN MIND

Not doing Our own will — Progress in the divine life — What we are saved unto — Living to please God — Loving the Word of God — Confession of failure — Wholly the Lord's. (page 157)

GEORGE MÜLLER'S EPITAPH
(page 167)

FOREWORD

"I live in the spirit of prayer. I pray as I walk about, when I lie down and when I rise up. And the answers are always coming. Thousands and tens of thousands of times have my prayers been answered. When once I am persuaded that a thing is right and for the glory of God, I go on praying for it until the answer comes." – *An Hour With George Müller, The Man of Faith to Whom God Gave Millions*, by Charles R. Parsons.

Over a hundred years after he spoke those words, the life of this man of prayer continues to strengthen the faithful and testify to all men the reality of the things of God. Born on September 27, 1805, George Müller showed the world that God answers prayer.

The well-known plight of children, and especially orphans, in nineteenth century England was widely described as a national disgrace at the time George Müller lived. In 1848, Lord Ashley referred to more than thirty thousand "naked, filthy, roaming lawless and deserted children, in and around the metropolis." Throughout the long reign of Queen Victoria, one-third of her subjects were under the age of fifteen. With a population that more than doubled in the 19th century, housing in the cities of England was scarce and expensive, and wages were kept down to a barely subsistence level.

Kellow Chesney described the situation as follows: "Hideous slums, some of them acres wide, some no more than crannies of obscure misery, make up a substantial part of the metropolis... In big, once handsome houses, thirty or more people of all ages may inhabit a single room."

The situation was exacerbated by the draconian New

Poor Law of 1834, which relegated the needy to prison-like institutions called workhouses, splitting up families and subjecting them to repugnant living conditions and hard labor. The Victorian era became notorious for the forced employment of children as young as four years old, often working sixteen hour days in factories and mines, where they generally died before the age of twenty-five. In 1834, in all of England there were accommodations for only 3,600 orphans. Twice that number of children under the age of eight was in prison, and only about twenty percent of the children in London had any schooling.

With only two shillings (less than fifty cents) in his pocket, but believing great enough to move mountains, George Müller set out to change things. As Roger Steer wrote in his biography, *George Müller, Delighted in God:*

> Müller's concern for the plight of orphans in nineteenth century England began rather more than a year before Dickens popularized the situation in Oliver twist. There can be no doubt either about the tragic proportions of the problem or that Müller's anxiety was genuine. When he first arrived in Bristol he was deeply moved by the common sight of children begging in the streets; and when they knocked on his own door he longed to do something positive to help....

> But there was another equally important reason why Müller contemplated founding an orphanage: he wanted to demonstrate to the world that there is a reality in the things of God. As he visited the members of his two congregations in Bristol he discovered repeatedly that people needed to have their faith strengthened.

> Müller longed for "... Something that would act as a visible proof that our God and Father is the same faithful God as ever He was; as willing has ever to

prove Himself to be the Living God, in our day as formerly, to all who put their trust in Him."

For the next sixty-four years of his life until his death at the age of ninety-two, Müller irrefutably proved God's sufficiency and care on a truly grand scale. Orphans were taken in without any charge for admission. They were well cared for, taught the Word of God, given a good education, and sent out into the world equipped with a trade to earn a good living. Starting with thirty children in one house, over the course of his lifetime Müller built five large buildings of solid granite, capable of accommodating two thousand orphans at a time. In total, he cared for 10,024 orphans in his life. Additionally, he also established 117 schools which provided a solid Christian education to over 120,000 children. Most astounding of all, though, is the way in which George Müller accomplished those deeds.

Müller looked to God alone to supply their every need. Along with everyone that worked for him, he operated under the maxim that no person was ever asked for anything, regardless of how great or pressing a need might appear. With unwavering trust in God, Müller daily prayed for the Lord to provide the food, clothing, and shelter for the thousands of children under his care; and God never failed them. They never missed a meal; they never lacked. From the minutely careful records Müller kept, it is evidenced that over the course of his life, over a 1,400,000 pounds ($7,000,000) were sent to him for the building and maintaining of these orphan homes in answer to prayer.

The undeniable reality of God's provision was evident to everyone familiar with the work. Samuel Chadwick in his book, *The Path of Prayer,* relates an occasion when Dr. A. T. Pierson was the guest of George Müller at his orphanage:

> One night when all the household had retired he [Müller] asked Pierson to join him in prayer. He told

him that there was absolutely nothing in the house for next morning's breakfast. My friend tried to remonstrate with him and to remind him that all the stores were closed. Müller knew all that. He had prayed as he always prayed, and he never told anyone of his needs but God. They prayed—at least Müller did—and Pierson tried to.

They went to bed and slept, and breakfast *for two thousand children was there in abundance at the usual breakfast hour.* Neither Müller nor Pierson ever knew how the answer came. The story was told next morning to Simon Short of Bristol, under pledge of secrecy until the benefactor died. The details of it are thrilling, but all that need be told here is that the Lord called him out of bed in the middle of the night to send breakfast to Müller's orphanage, and knowing nothing of the need, or of the two men at prayer, he sent provisions that would feed them a month.

Considering the extraordinary power in the prayer life of George Müller, it would be easy for some to regard him as a man with some special "gift of faith." Müller himself, however, was quick to correct that misconception. In 1869, Müller wrote:

> It is the selfsame faith which is found in every believer, and the growth of which I am most sensible of to myself; for, by little and little, it has been increasing for the last forty-three years. Oh! I beseech you, do not think me an extraordinary believer, having privileges above other of God's dear children, which they cannot have; nor look on my way of acting as something that would not do for other believers.

To those believers who desire to see for themselves that "God is faithful still, and hears prayer still," George Müller pointed them first to the Scriptures. There, he encouraged, they would come to know the loving Father who is always willing and able to supply our every need.

It is through the understanding of the Bible that Christians can learn how to get prayers answered and gain an accurate knowledge of faith. In the twentieth century, Dr. Victor Paul Wierwille, a great admirer of George Müller, taught people all over the world how to allow the Word of God to interpret itself, so that they too could see the power of God as Müller did. And through the ministry of Wierwille, a new generation of young men and women became familiar with, and affected by, the inspiring life of George Müller.

George Müller's life is remarkable not only for what he accomplished by speaking TO God, but also for what he accomplished in speaking ABOUT God. During the entire time Müller attended to the work of caring for thousands of orphans, he preached three times a week, totaling over 10,000 times. At the age of seventy, George Müller began to travel the world to preach, covering over 200,000 miles in forty-two different countries, and speaking in several different languages. For the next seventeen years, he preached on the average of once a day, frequently speaking to as many as 4,500 or 5,000 persons at a time, and reaching some three million people altogether.

George Müller had a profound impact on the lives of young believers, not only with the thousands of children he helped at the orphanages he founded, but also through the Word of God he shared in his extensive travels. While he spoke and wrote to believers young and old, new and seasoned; Muller felt especially drawn to those young in the faith. In the opening of *Counsel to Christians* he wrote, "… I have it specially on my heart to seek to lend a helping hand to young believers…they may be helped so to walk, that God may give them to enjoy peace and true happiness, and…to bear fruit to the praise, the honour, and glory of the

Lord." Here Müller shares the scriptures and his deep personal insight into God's heart to lead the new follower on the path to walking with God.

PREFACE

TO THE FIRST EDITION

These addresses were taken down by reporters, and afterwards, by request, revised by me. As it pleased the Lord greatly to bless them to many, not only at the time when they were delivered, but also when read in periodicals, it has appeared well to me to give them now to the public in this form. May the Lord condescend to let His blessing further rest upon them.

April 15th, 1878.

GEORGE MÜLLER.

Permanent Address,
New Orphan Houses, No. 3,
Ashley Down, Bristol.

COUNSELS TO CONVERTS
I

In leaving home to preach the Word of life, as it may please God to give openings to me, I have it specially on my heart to seek to. lend a helping hand to young believers, and to throw out points whereby, in the very outset of the Christian life, they may be helped so to walk, that God may give them to enjoy peace and true happiness, and which may, by His blessing, cause them in the very beginning of their spiritual life to bear fruit to the praise, the honour, and glory of the Lord. I more especially seek to do so, because, for the first four years after my conversion, I made many mistakes about the things of God, and was far from walking in the road which leads to real joy and happiness in the Lord, and far from being in a position to grow either in grace or knowledge.

READING THE SCRIPTURES

Four years after I had known the Lord, through the helping hand of an older and more experienced brother, I was led into a way whereby I increased more rapidly in knowledge and grace, and was consequently, in some little measure, able to glorify the Lord and to be more useful than before. The great mistake I made at the outset, was neglect of the divine Word, and in consequence of this many things were lacking. Therefore, it is laid upon my heart to impress it upon my younger brethren and sisters, to go from the very outset to the Word of God.

CONVICTION OF SIN

I now speak more especially to believers; and by this I do not understand those who at some time or other have had some religious impressions. These may lead to nothing, and therefore there must be something more in order to be children of God. In order to be believers in the Lord Jesus Christ, we must be regenerated, must be on the road to heaven, and have been "delivered from the power of darkness, and translated into the kingdom of His dear Son." For all this, more is wanted than mere religious impressions. Many persons have these, and are brought no further; but there they remain. It is needful that we should have been brought in a greater or less degree to look upon ourselves as sinners in need of a Saviour. And therefore I ask affectionately, Have we been convinced of this?

I am not speaking of degree. With ten thousand different persons, God may work in ten thousand different ways. I myself had little of this serious, deep conviction of sin at the beginning of my new life, and yet was, I believe, really and truly converted; and from the very beginning there was a marked difference in me. Yet I did see I was a sinner deserving punishment and nothing else. As to the degree of this sorrow, that is quite a different thing. We must, if we are children of God, have been convinced in the light of His word, that we are sinners deserving of punishment, and that the Lord Jesus Christ alone can save.

TRUST IN CHRIST

Then, again, we must be led to trust in Him; for we may have been convinced of sin, and yet have gone no further. If so, we are not on the road to heaven yet. We must have put all our trust in the Lord Jesus Christ for the salvation of our souls.

And all the more do I make these remarks, my beloved friends, because at such a time, when a wave of divine blessing has been passing through the land, and so many have been led to make a profession of faith, many may be trusting in a mere impression, perhaps a conviction, to some extent, of sin. All this is right as far as it goes, but not enough. Such are as yet in the state of which the Lord speaks—"Not far from the kingdom of heaven," and yet not in it. We must have passed from death unto life, ere we are the children of God, and there is no such thing as being a child of God without faith in the Lord Jesus Christ.

This, then, is most important, that we trust in Him, and in Him alone, for the salvation of our souls, and that we have no other hope in the matter of our salvation, than the merits and the intercession of Him, who sits on the right hand of God.

If we have been convinced of sin, and have believed in Him, then, as it is said in Acts 10:43, we have received remission of sin. Then are we the children of God, as in Gal. 3:26. And, again, it is said that "to as many as received" the Lord Jesus Christ, "to them gave He power to become the sons of God." It is to these poor sinners who have trusted in the Lord Jesus for the salvation of their souls, that I desire particularly to speak. Those alone are they who have the bright blessed prospect of heaven, and who know in their own blessed experience, the joy of the latter part of Rom. 8, or have the glorious confidence of Philippians 1:6, that "He who hath begun a good work will perform it." To you, brother and sister in Christ, I desire to say a few words as to the Christian life.

UPRIGHTNESS

One of the most deeply important points to the young believer—indeed to all believers—is, to aim after uprightness and honesty of heart. We may have a fair amount of prayerfulness, may read the word of God, may be frequently in a place of worship, and yet, with all these things, we lack much, yea all, if we have not uprightness of heart before God. My dear Christian friends, ask yourselves, as before God the Searcher of hearts, before Him who knows everything about you, how it is with you as to this point? Can you stand before Him, and say in honesty, "Lord, Thou knowest all things, Thou knowest that I love Thee, and that my desire is not to listen to sin and temptation, and not willingly to go on in anything contrary to Thy mind. I would have nothing that Thou hatest; but, by Thy grace, I am engaged in a warfare against it. Thou knowest how Thy weak, erring child hates the deeds of darkness, and desires to carry on a warfare daily against these powers."

Do we really seek to walk in this way? Then we shall have part in the blessed words of the Lord Jesus (Matt. 13:12), "Whosoever hath, to him shall be given, and he shall have more abundance."

I desire these words to be fixed upon your hearts, because, in looking back on the past fifty years, during which I have known the Lord, I can see the faltering steps with which I began. How weak I was! How ignorant! Even when preaching the Word, how ignorant! Although Christ was in me, the hope of glory, yet I failed again and again. Nevertheless, I made warfare against sin, and sought not to listen to Satan. I experienced, therefore, the truth of these words, "To Him that hath shall be given," and although it was by little and little, yet I did grow. So this evening I say to you, "Whosoever hath, to him shall be given, and he shall have more abundance."

But remember, it is added, "But whosoever hath not" —or only appears to have—"from him shall be taken away even that which he hath." Thus, those who do not maintain an upright heart, and who do not walk sincerely before God, shall, for the time, make no progress in the divine life, because the Holy Spirit does not work in such. Therefore it is deeply important to be sincere and honest before Him who knoweth the heart; and then, although we may be weak, yet we shall be helped in the divine life.

I know how much this one thing helped me at the first—honesty and uprightness of heart. And I remember one who was converted at the same time, and whom I met years after, and found he was just the same as at first—he had made no progress whatever; and it was because he was not honest and upright before God.

DENYING UNGODLINESS

The next deeply important point is this, whatever at the very outset of the divine life is hateful to God, must be given up. Whatever is offensive to Him, must be forsaken. Some say this is only needful regarding glaring sins, but it must be in everything. If the Holy Ghost says "No," the sin must be put aside at once. We must be faithful to Him. This unfaithfulness, this dallying with sin, is hindering the spiritual life of many. I wish to impress it on your hearts, that from the very beginning you should seek to be out-and-out Christians.

With many who set out in the divine life, the question is, "How much of the world can I keep, and yet get to heaven?" "How much can I enjoy of this world, and yet be saved?" There may be such a thing as being saved under such circumstances; but it is being saved "as by fire; "and none of God's children should be content to be saved as by fire.

Better far that you and I were to be at once taken home to the Lord, than that we should be satisfied with being saved ourselves, and still seeking to enjoy the fleeting pleasures of this world as much as possible; trying how much we can make of both worlds. This is the most wretched possible thing for us to do. Under such circumstances you will have just religion enough to make you a miserable Christian; a happy Christian you can never be while living so.

There are no happy children who are not also holy children. The Father says, "Let *that* mind be also found in you which was found in Him." And what was the life of the Lord Jesus? "Holy, harmless, undefined, and separate from sinners." His life was one single sacrifice to God, one single act of obedience to God. Now, we are left here to be representatives of the Lord Jesus Christ in this world. This great honour He has bestowed upon us here. He might bring us to know Him, and then take us away at once to be with Him, as with the thief on the cross; but, as you all know, this is not His ordinary way. He brings us to Himself, in order that "we may bring honour to His name, and glorify Him on this earth; and also, that we may practically and experimentally be prepared for the glory that awaits us above; and that each of us may have the honour of winning souls for Him, and be helpful to the children of God: in short, that we should bear fruit.

FRUITFULNESS

Well, this being the case—that we are left here to bring glory to His name—our heavenly Father expects us to live in separation from the world; and He does expect us not to go on in a sinful state. If we seek it, He will help us to be holy children, in order that we may be useful. Let us all aim after this. We should not be satisfied without bearing fruit, but should seek to be out-and-out for God.

There is such a thing as bearing much fruit—sixty or even a hundred-fold. Nor should you and I be content with thirty-fold, without seeking to bring forth sixty or a hundred-fold. Ought we not in earnest longing to pray that we may be permitted to bear fruit to the praise, honour, and glory of God?

But in order to this, there is nothing better than at once, in the very outset of the divine life, to aim after being out-and-out Christians. And never should any child of God harbour such a thought as this, "How much can I enjoy this world, and yet get to heaven at last? Is it possible for me by going to a ball, and attending a concert, or going to the theatre now and then, at last to get to heaven?" Oh! wretched, miserable state for a child of God to be in. Away with it! Be it far from any of those whom God has left on earth as witnesses for His glory.

I am here a pilgrim and a stranger, and far be it from me so to set my heart on this earth. I am going to heaven; this is not my place. As a child of God, I know that no place is my place save that upon which I can ask my Father's blessing. How could I ask His blessing in the theatre? How could I ask God to bless me in the whirl of the ball-room, or at the card-table, or in the noisy tavern? Away with all of them; they are the sinful pleasures of this evil world.

LIVING CHRIST

So, my beloved younger brethren and sisters in Christ at the very outset of your spiritual life, say boldly, "I will be, by the grace of God, an out-and-out Christian, living for God. I will, by His grace, seek to bear fruit to His glory and honour. I will, by His grace, seek to have done with this sinful world. I will, by His grace, strive so to live, that a line of demarcation shall be clearly seen between me and the world, and that the people of the world shall seek to have no intercourse with me, seeing that I do not belong to them, but that I belong to the kingdom of heaven."

That is what we have to aim after; and what would be the result? Not only should we be holy men and women, but also happy men and women, in whom God delights; and we should also be useful men and women. The world ought to say of each of us, "If ever there was a Christian, it is surely that man or that woman." "Surely that man or woman has been with Jesus." If the world does not say that of us, there is something wanting. We ought to be ashamed, if any one is able to live three or four days in the house with us, without finding out that we are not of the world, but are born again.

And that is not the only use of thus bearing testimony; it will also be very helpful to our brethren in the Lord.

Let me insist particularly, my beloved brethren and sisters, but especially you, my younger brethren and sisters, on this point—that of being out-and-out for God in the very outset. We must be opposed to the world, and the flesh, and entirely for Christ. This is the purpose for which we are left in the world. I do not say we are to give up our ordinary business. I have seen much of this; there is often too much readiness in giving up the earthly business, and it is often done hastily. I have found that men may greatly glorify God in their earthly business, and I do not say that they are to forsake that business in order to become evangelists, missionaries, district visitors, tract distributors, or the like. We may serve and honour Him well whilst occupied with the business of this life. If God does call us, by all means go at once; but do not go unless He calls. We require a special call from God, and even when we think we have received it, let us make it a matter of consideration. Let us prayerfully, quietly, and calmly look to God before taking such a step.

But, again, I say, if there be anything, whatever it may be, and however dear it may be, which is contrary to the divine will, let us give it up at once, and aim after being out-and-out, and decided for God in every way. The result will be increased happiness, joy, and holiness; and our usefulness will increase more and more.

In connection with this, I would especially state that, though we all ought to aim after conformity to the mind of Christ, yet we all more or less fail.

It is deeply important to mark, that all of us are liable to sin, and do sin. If any man come to me, and say, "I do not sin," I would say, "My brother, you are mistaken; perhaps you do not know what sin is, or you do not know your own state." All of us, though not living in sin, are yet liable to sin; if not in acts, yet in words; or if not even in words, yet in feelings or desires. We are all apt to fall short of what we might be and of what we ought to be. What then? Well, we must make confession, and come afresh to the blood of Jesus Christ, and have these sins washed away.

CONFESSION AND FORGIVENESS

Many children of God err here. As, for instance, when I was first converted, I thought, when I sinned that now it was all over, as I could not be a Christian, or a child of God. Or, if not this, there was at least a feeling in me, "Before you come to God in prayer, you must seek to be better." What a great mistake! And yet many of God's dear children make this mistake, and if they fall in any way, in acting, speaking, thinking, or desiring, they feel that they cannot approach with confidence.

What ought they to do? Why, at once to make confession to God. They should seek to enter into that gracious promise, "If we confess our sins, God is faithful and just to forgive us our sins." This is deeply important to us all, because the Spirit of God will not work in our hearts if there is guilt. There is therefore no practical power to resist sin, or to walk with God, as long as sin is not cleansed away. And as we are liable to err, more especially our younger brethren and sisters, yet we must not think we are not Christians because we do so-and-so. Let us cast away this thought, and not entertain it for a moment. Only let us be stirred to go afresh to the Lord Jesus Christ, to have the sin put away.

This is where the words of the Lord Jesus come in. "He that is washed needeth not save to wash his feet, but is clean every whit." Remember our position: we are not criminals; we were that, but such is not the case now. We are in the relationship of children. In this new relationship, however, we are apt to defile ourselves; just as a man who takes a bath in the morning, may require to wash his hands or his face throughout the day, and yet his body is clean. So are we, though apt to defile ourselves, yet clean.

But for this defilement we must come afresh, practically and experimentally, to the blood of Christ. If this be neglected, the result will be loss of power and joy. But it is a grievous mistake to stay away from God because we have sinned, and to wait until we are better. We are to come as we are, to obtain peace and joy in the Lord.

CONFESSING CHRIST

The next point is also deeply important, and it is, at the very outset of the divine life we must make a plain, bold confession of the Lord Jesus Christ. Very few things are of greater importance than this. The temptation will be, to keep your new life to yourself: "I can get to heaven without telling." Well, if you do so, you are weak, and will remain weak. It is of great importance, even for the vigour of your own Christian life, to make confession, and come out boldly for Christ at once. The reason is this —people will know that you are on the Lord's side, and will therefore no longer tempt you to act otherwise. They will no longer come with invitations to the theatre, or such and such a ball, or company, of a purely worldly character. You escape all this by open confession. If they know you are the Lord's, and see the line of demarcation between you and the world, they will not seek your company.

I remember when I was converted, I was a student in a large university, where there were twelve hundred and sixty students. Amongst all these there were only three who were known as disciples of the Lord Jesus Christ; but it was well known what they were; they were "marked men." I joined them, and became a "marked man" instantaneously. But we held out, and soon there were about half-a-dozen united together. We were called fanatics and mystics; and I used to be pointed at by my fellow-students, "There goes the mystic." What of this? In three or four weeks it was all over, and they left me alone. Before my conversion, I had been one of the gayest among them, and was continually at the theatre. If there was a ball, I was there; and in the tavern

I was one of the noisiest. But now, looked on as a "marked man," they gave me up as a hopeless case, and ceased to annoy me. Thus I escaped a thousand temptations to which I would otherwise have been exposed. If I had kept back the knowledge of my conversion, would I not have been continually tempted to sin?

This is my own experience; I know the blessed result of thus boldly confessing Christ, and would affectionately press it upon all my brothers and sisters in Jesus. If any here have not yet made this bold confession of then decision for Christ, oh, make it now! It will be of immense service to you.

Again, in doing so, we stand by the side of Christ. He comes forward, and takes His stand by our side, saying, "In weakness thou hast stood for Me; now I will stand by thee;" and thus we reap the benefit in our own souls. We can never have grace and strength by keeping our religion to ourselves. You will never be out-and-out Christians—never be happy Christians—without this confession.

The will of the Lord is that we should be as cities set on a hill, which cannot be hid; or as lights, not placed under a bushel, but set on a lamp-stand, so as to be seen. And, let us aim after this, if it is not the case with us now; and let us be assured, that, when any man aims at keeping his religion to himself, he is going the wrong road. People must know that we are the Lord's, and on His side; and we should not rest satisfied without this. Our duty, remember, is to win souls for Him; and how can we do this, if we hide our light? Although we are neither evangelists, missionaries, Sunday-school teachers, nor visitors, yet God will help us to win souls; therefore, we have to come out boldly for Him.

GROWTH IN CHRIST

Another deeply important point is this; very frequently the dear children of God, at the very outset of their new life, are immensely discouraged, because they do not feel themselves making the progress they ought to make, or wish to make. They are afraid, because they do not make this progress in knowledge or grace, that they are not Christians. Now, as an encouragement to the dear young brethren and sisters, I would say, be not over-discouraged by this. I do not mean to say we are to rest content without making progress, I only warn you against one of Satan's devices—viz., that when we are failing in any way, he is apt to say to us that we are not Christians; that, after all we have felt, we are only deceiving ourselves. Now, every one of you know well enough whether you are deceiving yourselves or not. You have all of you the witness within you, and you can look up and say, "Lord, Thou knowest all things; Thou knowest that I love Thee." We may not have the bold faith and triumphant assurance of Peter, or of Paul, but we can say "We do love Thee." And while conscious of our weakness and unworthiness, yet we are also conscious of our faith.

You know very well, for instance, when the child is born, it is not at once a young man. It is a babe; a weak, helpless babe. When it is a week old, you do not expect it to run about. We all know how it takes week after week, and month after month, ere it can so run. So it is in the divine life; you do not at once become young men or women in the Lord Jesus. And if any should come to me after being only three or four weeks in Christ, and complain that he is not full grown, I should say to him, " My dear friend, you are greatly mistaken; I do not expect to see you already become a young man, and far less a father in Christ." There is no such thing as fits and starts in the divine life. As in the natural life it requires some time to attain to manhood, so in the spiritual life; therefore let them not be discouraged that they have not yet become young men or young women in Christ, and far less that they have not become fathers and mothers in Him.

Let them, I say, not be discouraged, but steadily and

quietly go on, living according to the light God has given them. If they are thus walking, it will be unto them according to the promise, "To him that hath, it shall be given, and be shall have more abundance." For your encouragement, let me give you my own experience.

OLD ENEMIES

I was, at the beginning of my new life, again and again overcome by my old tendencies. For instance, I had been a habitual liar in former days, and could stand and look people in the face, and deliberately say things that were not true. If any of you have been so, my friends, you know what a terrible thing it is. Well, after my conversion I stated twice things that were not true; but that was a very different thing from habitually telling lies; for with sorrow of heart I confessed it before God, and owned before Him that such and such was not the truth.

Again, I had been a habitual attendant at the theatre; and twice after my conversion, through circumstances, I was drawn in to go to the theatre; but, nevertheless, I was humbled before the Lord, and it was a very different thing from my former habitual attendance.

Soon God delivered me from that also. Therefore I wish to say that no child of God who, by deeds, words, or thoughts, is carried away to sin against God, should give heed to the suggestion of the devil, "There is no reality in your conversion." Rather let us come afresh to the blood of Jesus, which "taketh away all sin." Remember that this blood not only washes away, but also gives us more and more power over sin. By coming frequently, we shall grow in grace and in experience. I may say I have grown somewhat since those days, to which, for your encouragement, I have referred; and what one has done, others may do.

CHURCH FELLOWSHIP

Another important point is, to seek at once, or as soon

as possible, to unite ourselves to some dear children of God, or to some faithful ministry. Wherever you find Christians, with whom it would be to your profit to mingle, or a ministry likely to feed your soul, go there; only get into some little band of God's children, or disciples, at once. Remember, it will be very helpful to you in your new life.

I am not referring to this or that particular place, but wherever God has cast your lot, and wherever there are dear children of the Lord, go there. Go where the gospel is faithfully set forth, and get united to them, that they may help you as the younger brother or sister. You will find such fellowship very helpful to you. I myself found it of the utmost value.

Shortly after my conversion, there were a few other students led to the Lord, and we used to meet together regularly in my room, and sought to help one another. It was very helpful. But, where practicable, I would advise you to seek out the company of some older and more experienced Christian—one who is really a living gospel Christian—to whom you can speak freely, and from whom you can get much useful advice and counsel. All you older believers may lend a helping band to your younger brothers and sisters, and thus be a great help to one another.

I have often found that, when led astray by natural tendency, the fellowship of my brother-students was exceedingly helpful, and often brought me into the light again. Especially would I say to all Christians—not merely the younger, but even the older—seek to have some truly spiritual friend, to whom you can run and unbosom yourself, and take sweet counsel together; you will find it to be very helpful in the things of God.

I have much more to say, but will continue the subject on Friday evening, when I will seek to bring before you many other important points.

COUNSELS TO CONVERTS
II

As most of you know already, the especial object of our meeting is, to continue the subject of last Tuesday evening. On that evening, I sought to lend a helping hand to beloved Christian friends, specially the younger brothers and sisters, who are setting out in the divine life.

As one who for fifty years has known the Lord, and has laboured in word and doctrine, I ought to be able, in some little measure, to lend a helping hand to these younger believers. And, by the grace of God, I can say, I *am* able to lend this helping hand; that is, if God will only condescend to use my own failures, to which I have freely referred, and my experience, as a help to others in walking on the road to heaven, I trust that your coming here will not be in vain. As I already told you, this was the very purpose of my leaving home, that I might help these dear young brethren.

I have already referred to seven different points, which appealed to me to be of great moment. There still remain, however, some other deeply important ones to be considered.

THE MANNER OF READING THE WORD

One of the most deeply important points is, that of attending to the careful, prayerful reading of, and meditation on the word of God. I would ask your particular attention to one verse in the epistle of Peter (1 Peter 2:2) where we are especially exhorted by the Holy Ghost, through the apostle, regarding this. For the sake of the connection, let us read the first verse, "Wherefore laying aside all malice, and all guile, and hypocrisies, and envies, and all evil speaking, as new born babes, desire the sincere milk of the Word, that ye may grow thereby; if so be ye have tasted that the Lord is gracious."

The particular point to which I refer is contained in the second and third verses, "as new born babes, desire the sincere milk of the Word." As growth in the natural life is attained by proper food, so in the spiritual life, if we desire to grow, this growth is only to be attained through the instrumentality of the word of God. It is not stated here, as some might be very willing to say, "the reading of the Word may be of importance under some circumstances." That you may gain more by reading this tract, or this and that book, is not the statement here; it is "the Word," and nothing else, and, under all circumstances,

STICK TO THE WORD OF GOD

You say that the reading of this tract or that book often does you good. I do not question it at all. Nevertheless, the instrumentality which God has been pleased to appoint and use is that of the Word itself; and just in the measure in which the disciples of the Lord Jesus Christ attend to this, they will become strong in the Lord; and in so far as it is neglected, so far will they be weak. There is such a thing as babes being neglected, and what is the consequence? They never become healthy men or women, because of that early neglect.

Perhaps—and it is one of the most hurtful forms of this neglect—they obtain improper food, and therefore do not attain to the full vigour of manhood or womanhood. So with regard to the divine life. It is a most deeply important point, that we obtain right spiritual food at the very beginning of that life. What is that food? It is "the sincere milk of the Word;" that is the proper nourishment for the strengthening of the inner man. Listen, then, my dear brethren and sisters, to this advice with regard to the Word.

CONSECUTIVE READING

First of all, it is of the utmost moment that we regularly read through the Scripture. We ought not to turn over the Bible, and pick out chapters as we please here and there, but to read it regularly through. We should read carefully and regularly through the Scriptures. I speak advisedly, and as one who has known the blessedness of thus reading the Word for the last forty-six years. I say *forty-six* years, because for the first four years of my Christian life I did not carefully read the word of God. I used to read a tract, or an interesting book; but I knew nothing of the power of the Word. I read next to nothing of it, and the result was, that, though a preacher then, and though I had preached in connection with the establishment again and again, yet I made no progress in the divine life. And why? Just for this reason, that I neglected the word of God.

But it pleased God, through the instrumentality of a beloved Christian brother, then labouring in this very city and neighbourhood, with whom I became acquainted in Devonshire, to rouse in me an earnestness about the Word, and ever since then I have been a lover of it.

Let me, then, press upon you my first point, that of attending regularly to reading through the Scripture. I do not suppose that you *all* need the exhortation: many, I believe, have already done so, but I speak for the benefit of those who have not. To those I say, my dear friends, begin at once. Begin with the Old Testament, and when you have read a chapter or two and are about to leave off, put a mark that you may know where you have left off. I speak in all simplicity, for the benefit of those who may be young in the divine life. The next time you read, begin the New Testament, and again put a mark where you leave off. And thus go on always, whether in the Old or New Testaments, putting in a mark, and reading alternately the Old and the New Testaments. Thus, by little and little, you will read through the whole Bible; and when you have finished, just begin again at the beginning.

THE CONNECTION OF SCRIPTURE

Why is this so deeply important? Simply that we may see the connection between one book and another of the Bible, and between one chapter and another. If we do not read in this consecutive way, we lose a great part of what God has given to instruct us. Moreover, if we are children of God, we should be well acquainted with the whole revealed will of God—the whole of the Word. "All Scripture is given by inspiration, and is profitable."

And much may be gained by thus carefully reading through the whole will of God. Suppose a rich relative were to die, and leave us, perhaps, some land, or houses, or money, should we be content with reading only the clauses that affected us particularly? No, we would be careful to read the whole will right through. How much more, then, in the will of God, ought we to be careful to read it right through, and not merely one and another of the chapters or books.

BENEFIT OF CONSECUTIVE READING

And this careful reading of the word of God has this advantage, that it keeps us from making a system of doctrines of our own, and from having our own particular favourite views, which is very pernicious. We often are apt to lay too much stress on certain views of the truth which affect us particularly. The will of the Lord is, that we should know His whole mind. Again, variety in the things of God is of great moment. And God has been pleased to give us this variety in the highest degree; and the child of God, who follows out this plan, will be able to take an interest in any part of the Word.

Suppose one says, "Let us read, in Leviticus." Very well, my brother. Suppose another says, "Let us read in the prophecy of Isaiah." Very well, my brother. And another will say, "Let us read in the gospel according to Matthew." Very well, my brother; I can enjoy them all; and whether it be in the Old Testament, or in the New Testament, whether in the prophets, the gospels, the Acts, or the Epistles, I should welcome it, and be delighted to welcome the reading and study of any part of the divine Word.

A SPECIAL BENEFIT

And this will be particularly of advantage to us, in case we should become labourers in Christ's vineyard; because, in expounding the Word, we shall be able to begin at the beginning. We shall equally enjoy the reading of the Word, whether of the Old or the New Testament, and shall never get tired of it. I have, as before stated, known the blessedness of this plan for forty-six years, and though I am now nearly seventy years of age, and though I have been for nearly fifty years in the divine life, I can say, by the grace of God, that I more than ever love the word of God, and have greater delight than ever in reading it.

And this day, though I have read the Word nearly a hundred times right through, I am as fond as ever of reading the Scripture; I never have got tired of reading it, and this is more especially through reading it regularly, consecutively day by day, and not merely reading a chapter here and there, as my own thoughts might have led me to do.

READING THE WORD PRAYERFULLY

Again, we should read the Scripture prayerfully, never supposing that we are clever enough, or wise enough, to understand God's Word by our own wisdom. In all our reading of the Scriptures let us seek carefully to have the help of the Holy Spirit; let us ask, for Jesus' sake, that He will enlighten us; He is willing to do it.

I will tell you how it fared with me, at the very first; it

may be for your encouragement. It was in the year 1829, when I was living in Hackney, not far from here. My attention had been called to the teaching of the Spirit by a dear brother of experience. "Well," I said, "I will try this plan; and will give myself to the careful reading and meditation of the word of God after prayer, and I will see how much, the Spirit is willing to teach me in this way."

AN ILLUSTRATION OF THIS

I went accordingly to my room, and locked my door, and putting the Bible on a chair, I went down on my knees at the chair. There I remained for several hours in prayer and meditation over the word of God; and I can tell you that I learned more in those three hours which I spent in this way, than I had learned for many months previously. I found the blessing was so great, that all the manuscripts, which I had written down from the lectures of the professors of Divinity in the university that I previously attended, I now considered to be of so little value, that when, soon after, I moved into Devonshire, I did not think them worth the carriage. This was because I now found the Holy Spirit to be a better teacher than professors of Divinity. I obtained the teaching of the divine Spirit, and I cannot tell you the blessedness it was to my own soul. I was praying in the Spirit, and putting my trust in the power of the Spirit as I had never done before.

You cannot, therefore, be surprised at my earnestness in pressing this upon you, when you have heard how precious to my heart it was, and how much it helped me.

MEDITATE ON THE WORD

But again, it is not enough to have prayerful reading only, but we must also meditate on the Word. As in the instance I have just referred to, kneeling before the chair, I meditated on the Word; not simply reading it, not simply praying over it; all that, but, in addition, pondering over what I had read. This is deeply important. If you merely read the Bible, and no more, it is just like water running in at one side and out at the other. In order to be really benefitted by it, we must meditate on it.

Not all of us, of course, can spend many hours, or even one or two hours, each day thus. Our business demands our attention. Yet, however short the time you can afford, give it regularly to reading, prayer, and meditation over the Word, and you will find it well repaid.

MAKE THE MEDITATION PERSONAL

In connection with this, we should always read and meditate over the word of God, with reference to ourselves and our own heart. This is deeply important, and I cannot press it too earnestly upon you. We are apt often to read the Word with, reference to others. Parents read it in reference to their children, children for their parents, evangelists read it for their congregations, Sunday-school teachers for their classes. Oh! this a poor way of reading the Word; read so it will not profit. I say it deliberately and advisedly, the sooner it is given up, the better for your own souls. Read the word of God always with reference to your own heart, and when you have received the blessing in your own heart, you will be able to communicate it to others.

Whether you labour as evangelists, as pastors, or as visitors, superintendents of Sunday schools, or teachers, tract distributors, or in whatever other capacity you may seek to labour for the Lord, be careful to let the reading of the Word be with distinct reference to your own heart. Ask yourselves, How does this suit me, either for instruction, for correction, for exhortation, or for rebuke? How does this affect me? If you thus read, and get the blessing in your own soul, how soon will it flow out to others.

READ IN FAITH

Another point. It is of the utmost moment in reading the word of God, that the reading should be accompanied with faith. "The word preached did not profit them, not being mixed with faith in them that heard it." As with the preaching, so with the reading—it must be mixed with faith. Not simply reading it as you would read a story, which you may receive or not: not simply as a statement, which you may credit or not, or as an exhortation, to which you may listen or not; but as the revealed will of the Lord: that is, receiving it with faith. Received thus, it will nourish us, and we shall really reap benefit. Only in this way will it benefit us; and we shall gain from it health and strength, in proportion as we receive it with real faith.

BE DOERS OF THE WORD

Lastly, if God does bless us in reading His word, He expects that we should be obedient children, and that we should accept the Word as His will, and carry it into practice. If this be neglected, you will find that the reading of the Word, even if accompanied by prayer, meditation, and faith, will do you little good. God does expect us to be obedient children, and will have us practice what He has taught us. The Lord Jesus Christ says: "If ye know these things, happy are ye if ye do them," And in the measure in which we carry out what our Lord Jesus taught, so in measure are we happy children. And in such measure only can we honestly look for help from the Father, even as we seek to carry out His will.

If there is one single point I would wish to have spread all over this country, and over the whole world, it is just this, that we should seek, beloved Christian friends, not to be hearers of the Word only, but doers of the Word. I doubt not that many of you have sought to do this already, but I speak particularly to those younger brethren and sisters who may not yet have learned the full force of this. Oh, seek to attend earnestly to this; it is of vast importance. Satan will seek with much earnestness to put aside the word of God; but let us seek to carry it out and to act upon it. The

Word must be received as a legacy from God, which we have by the Holy Ghost.

THE FULNESS OF THE REVELATION GIVEN IN THE WORD

And remember that, to the faithful reader of this blessed Word, it reveals all that we need to know of the Father—all that we need to know about the Lord Jesus Christ, all about the power of the Spirit, all about the world that lieth in the wicked one, all about the road to heaven, and the blessedness of the world to come. In this blessed book we have the whole gospel, and all rules necessary for our Christian life and warfare. Let us see, then, that we study it with our whole heart, and with prayer, meditation, faith, and obedience.

PRAYER

The next point on which I will speak for a few moments, has been more or less referred to already; it is that of prayer. You might read the Word and seem to understand it very fully, yet, if you are not in the habit of waiting continually upon God, you will make little progress in the divine life. We have not naturally in us any good thing, and cannot expect, save by the help of God, to please Him. Therefore, it is the will of the Lord, that we should always own our dependence upon Him, and it becomes us to follow in prayer the earnestness of the Lord Jesus Christ.

That blessed One gave us an example in this particular, He gave whole nights to prayer, and we find Him on the lonely mountain engaged by night in prayer. And as in every way He is to be an example to us, so, in particular, on this point, He is also an example to us. The old evil, corrupt nature is still in us, though we are born again; therefore we have to come in prayer to God for help. We have to cling to the power of the Mighty One. Concerning everything we have to pray. Not simply when great troubles come, when our house is on fire, or our beloved wife is on the point of death, or our dear children are laid down in sickness, not simply at such times, but also in little things. From the very early morning, let us make everything a matter of prayer, and let it be so throughout the day, and throughout our whole life.

A Christian lady said, lately, that thirty-five years ago she heard me speak on this subject in Devonshire; and that then I referred to praying about little things. I had said, that suppose a parcel came to us, and it should prove difficult to untie the knot, and you cannot cut it; then you should ask God to help you, even to untie the knot. I myself had forgotten the words, but she has remembered them, and the remembrance has been a great help to her again and again. So I would say to you, my beloved friends, there is nothing too small for prayer. In the simplest things connected with our daily life and walk, we should give ourselves to prayer; and we shall have the living, loving Lord Jesus to help us. Even in the most trifling matters I give myself to prayer, and often in the morning, even ere I leave my room, I have two or three answers to prayer in this way.

Young believers, in the very outset of the Divine life, learn, in childlike simplicity, to wait upon God for everything! Treat the Lord Jesus Christ as your personal Friend, able and willing to help you in everything. How blessed it is to be carried in His loving arms all the day long! I would say, that the divine life of the believer is made up of a vast number of little circumstances and little things. Every day there come before us a variety of little trials, and if we seek to put them aside in our own strength and wisdom, we shall quickly find that we are confounded. But if, on the contrary, we take everything to God, we shall be helped, and our way shall be made plain. Thus our life will be a happy life!

FAITH MUST COME FIRST

There are two passages in the word of God of the

deepest moment to Christians, and I would therefore speak on them. The first is in 2 Peter 1:5: "Besides this, add to your faith virtue," etc. It is here supposed that we have faith in the Lord Jesus Christ, because we are commanded to add to our faith virtue, and these other graces. The apostle Peter is addressing believers, and here to-night I am supposing that I am speaking to believers. Yet, peradventure, there may be some who are not believers. To you, if there be any such, I would say, you are sinners. You may be young in this life, or you may be advanced in years; yon may be very moral, or otherwise; but in the sight of God you are sinners. This you must, if you would be saved, realize and understand that you are sinners, and not only so, but sinners deserving punishment. You are lost, and have no power of your own to save yourselves. The world talks about turning over a new leaf, but that will not satisfy Divine justice. The record of your past sins stands against you, and must be blotted out.

What then? You are sinners, and sinners deserving of punishment, nothing but punishment. You must either suffer that eternal punishment yourselves, or obtain another to bear it. Well, the Lord Jesus Christ came into the world to bear this punishment. He has borne it in our room and stead. He has suffered for us. And now the only one thing that God looks for from the sinner is, that we should put our trust in the Lord Jesus Christ, and in Him alone, for the salvation of our souls. We must look entirely to Himself; we must look only to the blessed Lamb of God, who was nailed to the Cross. Whosoever trusteth in Him shall be saved. Let his sins be never so many, yet he shall have forgiveness for all his transgressions. He is born again—is regenerated, through faith in the Lord Jesus Christ. He will be made a child of God, an heir of God, and joint-heir with Christ. Thanks be to His came, "who hath delivered us from the power of darkness, and hath translated us into the kingdom of His dear Son."

If we have believed in the Lord Jesus, we are, however, not to be satisfied with this, but to seek to add to our faith virtue; and to virtue knowledge; and to knowledge temperance; and to temperance patience; and to patience godliness.

COURAGE

"Add to your faith virtue." "Virtue" here means fortitude, or courage; implying that the very first thing after believing on the Lord Jesus Christ, is, to own our attachment to Him. You must stand boldly out and make confession of Him. Some dear children of God think we may keep our religion to ourselves; there is no use in bringing it before our friends, companions, or relations—no use getting into trouble with them about it. What is the result? The Lord Jesus Christ will not stand on our side to strengthen us, if we will not take our stand by Him. Weak we are, weak we must remain, as long as we are in this state. I do not say you will go to hell. But you are half-hearted, and the Master wants valiant soldiers. He looks for fortitude. He will have us let those around us know whose we are, honestly and openly. Therefore we ought to be decided for Christ; that is of the utmost moment. The more we come out from the world, the better it will be for us in the things of God. We shall be strengthened, and the bolder we are for Christ, the happier will it be for ourselves. Let me impress this on the hearts of my younger brethren and sisters in Christ; and if they have not already done so, let them make confession of Christ.

KNOWLEDGE

"Add to your faith, virtue, and to virtue, knowledge." Here, again, we have something to learn. I have already spoken of the importance of reading and meditating on God's word; but here comes a special exhortation to add to your faith, knowledge. We are not to be satisfied with knowing that we are sinners, and that Christ is our Saviour, but we must seek to make progress in knowledge. Why is this? Because to increase in knowledge, is to increase in the knowledge of God. And as we increase in this knowledge of Him, we learn more and more of His love; and that it is the very joy of His heart to do us good. We see more and more what a lovely Being God is; and the result of this again is, that we are satisfied with His dealings with us.

I have passed through very many trials, some of them of no ordinary character; yet I have rejoiced in God. For nearly ten years—from 1838 to 1848—I had difficulty upon difficulty, scarcely anything but difficulty. But I had always the help of God, and always was joyous, even in the darkest day, because I knew that all came from God, my Father. On that account I say to you, seek to increase in knowledge; and then although there may fall upon you trial and affliction, even heavy trial, deep affliction, yet if you can say, "It is from my Father, my loving Father; from Him who spared not His Son for me, and from Him who hath said that He will make all things work together for good; having freely given up Jesus for me, He will freely give me all things; therefore this trial must be good for me, else He would not suffer it to befall me." You can easily see how in such a state of mind, we can pass through, these trials; and even in the midst of them we may have calmness and peace, and even holy heavenly joy. Thus we shall be able to meet them. That is the result of being really acquainted with God. And the only way to get this knowledge is, by diligent study of the Word, and by the teaching of the Spirit from that Word. Let us, therefore, aim after this knowledge, and not be satisfied with the simple belief that we shall get to heaven.

TEMPERANCE

The apostle next says, add to your faith temperance. Now this is not merely abstaining from excess in drinking—though it does mean that; but self-control generally is here the meaning of this word. That is, regarding everything, whether meat or drink, or any other thing, that we do not give way to the abuse of anything God has given us. It is here used as regarding our temper, appetites, and deportment generally. Because by the way in which we conduct ourselves, or behave ourselves, do we glorify God or dishonour Him. The world is watching us, to see how so-and-so, who has become a Christian, behaves himself. And if they see us walk inconsistently, then do they speak against our Master; while if, on the other hand, they see us walk consistently, they are compelled to give honour to our God.

PATIENCE

"And to temperance, patience;" that is, to be satisfied with the will of God. If we have this contentment, we shall be able to endure tribulation and suffering, and even bereavement and sickness, satisfied that it is for the best. If we are the children of God, we are but strangers and pilgrims here. This is not our home, we here have no abiding city; therefore we heed not the troubles or difficulties by the way, they will soon pass. Let us therefore aim after showing, by our quiet, patient demeanour, that we are satisfied with God.

GODLINESS

Add to your faith godliness, that is, the habit of referring everything to God. That we pray about everything and do everything as seeing Him who is above; that we walk as confident that God is our strength; that we walk by day and by night, as in the sight of God; in short, that we walk in holy, precious fellowship with God; that we remember that He is before us, and with us; that the Father's eye is upon us, and that we seek to be guided and directed in everything by Him. Oh that we might take up the meaning of all this, and carry it into our lives!

Now, my beloved Christian friends, is it your calm,

quiet purpose to aim after all this? If so, you may be certain that God will give you more power to follow Him. God allows us, for His own wise purpose, to have our lot in this life cast amidst darkness in many respects. But think not of that; remember, we are getting nearer the end. The day is drawing near when the Lord Jesus Christ will come. I do not say by this that I can specify the time, or that it will be such and such a date; I know nothing of the precise time. But this is certain, we are getting nearer,—nearer the end. Nearer the day when the Lord Jesus Christ will appear in glory to call His waiting saints to meet Him in the air.

How the thought ought to warm our hearts, and to fill us with a longing to serve Him, and to be like Him. If others are cold, then let us seek to warm them. If others are foolish, let us seek to teach them. If fire be lacking in others, let us, His servants, be burning coals to set them on fire. Let us remember, that it is more blessed to give than to receive. Oh, the blessedness of bearing much love to others, instead of receiving it only; of warming others instead of being warmed only; of teaching others instead of being taught ourselves only Oh, therefore, beloved in Christ, let it be a matter of great moment to you, that you aim after godliness, living near to God in this life, that we may enjoy the blessedness of being living witnesses for Him! Let us seek that we may be made burning coals; and if all the "brethren and sisters here were thus set on fire, how soon should we set Mildmay Park on fire. Then, would it not extend to Hackney? And then it would light up London itself. In helping to bless others we shall be greatly blessed in our own souls; and the fire thus kindled will burn in our own hearts. The passage which follows this contains so much that I will rather leave it for our next meeting.

COUNSELS TO CONVERTS
III

In seeking to lend a helping hand to my beloved fellow-disciples, especially the younger ones, I came, at our last meeting, to a portion of Scripture containing deeply important instruction, in connection with this subject. You will find it in 2 Pet.1, from the fifth verse. I will just read a few verses, for the sake of the connection, rip to the verse at which I left off.

I suppose, of course, that those whom I address are trusting in the atoning blood of the Lamb alone, for the salvation of their souls; but if any be present who know not the Saviour, may God in the riches of His grace stir them up to see the state in which they are by nature. "We are all sinners deserving punishment, and nothing but punishment, in the state in which we are by nature; and the only way we can escape it, is by having

A SUBSTITUTE

to bear the punishment. This substitute God has provided in the person of His only begotten Son, Jesus Christ, who has been punished in our room and stead, and whose perfect obedience unto death, even the death of the cross, has been accepted in the room of sinners, who, by trusting in Him alone, can obtain the salvation of their souls. All here present who have not yet trusted in Him, may cast themselves upon the mercy of God, by accepting what He has provided in the person and work of the Lord Jesus. Thus they would become like us, who have obtained forgiveness; would be delivered from the power of darkness, and translated into the kingdom of His dear Son; would be brought from darkness into light, and obtain peace to their souls; would be brought on the road to heaven, and made children of God, and joint-heirs with Christ; and would have the bright, blessed prospect of glory; and, while on the road to their home, would have a part in the intercession of the Lord Jesus Christ, who is at the right hand of God, and who is coming again to receive us to Himself, that where He is, there we may be also.

POINTS ALREADY CONSIDERED

Now, as I said before, I suppose that all present have believed on the Lord Jesus Christ; then are you doing as Peter writes, "Add to your faith virtue?" Again I mention that this word "virtue" is used in the sense of courage or fortitude, particularly implying that we are to make confession of Christ, and to stand out for Him, and boldly own Him before a wicked world.

Then, as I already observed, we are also to increase in knowledge, specially in the knowledge of the revelation which God has been pleased to make of Himself and His dear Son in the Holy Scriptures. This precious book shows to us the vanity of this world, and the blessedness and reality of heavenly things, and the joys that await us in the Father's house.

"And to knowledge, temperance." This means self-control; not merely to abstain from excess in drinking. It means far more, referring to our temper, way of life, our speech, and whole deportment; to be living in the world as becomes the children of God. And to this add patience; quietly waiting for God in the hour of trial and deep affliction, and expecting Him to deliver us.

And to this add godliness; that is, the habit in which everything is brought to God, and referred to Him; in which we seek to walk to the praise and honour and glory of God, and at all times and under all circumstances to make this our business—our especial business—to live for God and under the eye of God; and that we do not turn away our eyes from God, but that we seek to go straight on, walking with God all the day long; living, speaking, acting for Him; cultivating the precious habit in which we walk with and live for God.

Thus far we proceeded on the last evening. Now we come to

BROTHERLY KINDNESS;

that is, "the love of the brethren." That especially is to be aimed after, and if this is wanting, there is very much wanting. The heavenly Father looks for love among His children, whom He has loved with an eternal and unchangeable love. He would have us love one another. And if we do not love the brethren, where is the proof that we love God? God does specially look for this love, and He would have us add to all other graces, particularly this grace—the love of the brethren.

And more, we are to add to all this,

CHARITY;

that is, universal love. Not merely are we to love the children of God, but to love those who are not of us, and who do not love us. We are to love those who do not care in the least for us. We are to love those who do not walk with us on the road to heaven, and whom we have never even seen or heard of. We are to love every one of the human family; that is the will of our heavenly Father regarding us.

He would have the heart of His children so large as to take in all; and then we have what is commanded—universal love, which will manifest itself in seeking to do good to all our fellow-men.

We shall seek to do them good in every possible way, but specially in striving after the salvation of their souls. For this is what our heavenly Father teaches us, when He causes His sun to shine on the evil as well as on the good, and when His rain descends on the just and the unjust. By all this He would teach us to love everyone, even our enemies themselves. "To brotherly kindness, therefore, add charity"—love to all.

THE RESULT OF THIS—FRUIT

Now comes the next thing; what is the practical result of all this? It is fruit. "For if these things be in you and abound, they make you that ye shall neither be barren nor unfruitful in the knowledge of our Lord Jesus Christ."

If we seek to "add to our faith virtue, and to virtue knowledge, and to knowledge temperance, and to temperance patience, and to patience godliness, and to godliness brotherly kindness, and to brotherly kindness charity"; then, if these things be in us and abound, "we shall neither be barren nor unfruitful in the knowledge of our Lord Jesus Christ."

It is impossible to lead an idle life, if these things be found in us; for we shall be seeking to bring glory to God, and it is impossible that we should not bear fruit. If these things be found in us, it is impossible to stand still in the divine life; we shall surely make progress to the praise and honour and glory of God. We shall bear fruit. And the result will be that we shall not merely bear fruit thirty-fold, not merely forty-fold, or forty-fivefold, not even fifty, fifty-five, or sixty-fold only; but there is the possibility, even in this latter part of the nineteenth century, to bring forth fruit eighty or ninety-fold; and who shall tell us there is not even the possibility of bearing fruit a hundred-fold? But whether we do bear fruit to this extent or not, it should be our aim to bear fruit abundantly; and if we aim at sixty or seventy-fold, we may have a hundred-fold.

THE CONTRARY RESULT

But now notice:—"He that lacketh these things is blind, and cannot see afar off, and hath forgotten that he was purged from his old sins." That is the state of the man who does not seek to add to his faith these graces. "He that lacketh these things" (that is, he that neglecteth these things) "cannot see afar off" (that is, is dim-sighted).

It must be so, my brethren. He may have good natural sight, needing no spectacles; he may have clear judgment about business matters, and a thoroughly clear judgment of all temporal matters of this life; yet, if he does not seek to add to his faith all these things, he is dim-sighted, he has not spiritual judgment or discernment, and all his worldly wisdom is nothing. He becomes a hindrance to his fellow disciples instead of a helper; and instead of a counsellor to his younger brethren in Christ, he becomes a darkener of counsel. How deeply important, not to get into such a state, and therefore, my young brethren and sisters in Christ, I beseech you not to allow yourselves to become spiritually blind.

"And hath forgotten that he was purged from his old sins." What a sad thing if, after all that God has done for you, in bringing you to see that you are by nature sinners, in helping you to believe on the Lord Jesus Christ, so that your sins have been forgiven, and you have been delivered from the powers of darkness, and translated into the kingdom of His dear Son,—how if, after all this, you become blind, or dim-sighted, and your heavenly vision becomes obscured!

If our new light were to be darkened—those eyes which, by the power of the Spirit, have been enlightened—how sad it would he! If by reason of carelessness or worldly-mindedness, we should lose this spiritual sight, oh, how great the darkness would be! God's saints are all in danger of this. Not only until we have been believers ten, twenty, or thirty years, but as long as we are in the body, there is this danger. How deeply important, then, for us to take measures to be kept from this spiritual blindness!

Remember, then, that "he that lacketh these things is

blind." He has not the mind of God; he has more or less the mind of the world; and if you bring certain things before him, such as the importance of prayer, that man will probably say you are too religious, too pious; he cannot understand you. Why is all this? Why should a man who has been forgiven and placed on the road to heaven, whose eyes have been opened to spiritual things, become thus blind? It is by neglecting to add to his faith these graces, he has become dim-sighted concerning the heavenly realities; he has been spiritually blinded, and has forgotten the state from which he was delivered. How deeply important, therefore, that we should cultivate these graces! Very many of the dear children of God, who, at the commencement of their divine life saw clearly their state, that they were sinners, and deserving punishment, and who, through the blood of the Lord Jesus Christ, by faith in Him, had peace, and had known the enjoyment and blessedness of fellowship with God, by getting careless and worldly-minded, and by living to a greater or less degree under the influence of this world, have at last forgotten that their sins were all forgiven, and that they are the children of God.

Thus they lose all the blessed enjoyment of their position, as children of God and heirs of heaven; and what is the result of all this? They more and more settle down in this world, and become less and less spiritually-minded, and become more and more lovers of this world.

What a sad state is this, and oh! my beloved brethren, may God keep us all from falling into it. Therefore it is that I do desire to warn you against ceasing to add to your faith all those graces: virtue, knowledge, temperance, patience, godliness, brotherly-kindness, and charity. All these things are to be added.

And now, "Wherefore, the rather." That is, because of all that has been said, we are to aim after "giving all diligence, to

MAKE OUR CALLING AND ELECTION SURE."

Have we all done this? Is it true of you all, my beloved brothers and sisters in Christ, that you have made your calling and election sure? Is it as certain with you all, that you will go to heaven, as if you were there already?

"But," you say, "how can we do this?" Just by attending to the points brought before us in the previous verses. For if we attend to all these things, then we shall make our calling and election sure. We shall have the assurance in our own soul, that we are the children of God; that we have received the forgiveness of sins, and that our Father loves us; that we are on the road to heaven, and that we have before us the bright and blessed prospect of glory, and are daily getting "nearer home"; and that we shall most assuredly reach heaven at last.

In order to have this blessed assurance let us, my beloved brethren, aim after all these things, that we may make our calling and election sure.

There is such a thing as doing this. I should be doing dishonour to my God, and failing in my duty, if I did not bear witness to-day that I have made my calling and election sure. After having been about fifty years a believer, I bear testimony that I know I am a child of God, that I have been forgiven, and that I am on the road to heaven. And although, in myself, nothing but a poor, weak, miserable sinner, and though if I had only committed the fiftieth part of the sins I have been guilty of, I know I should deserve punishment—nothing but punishment; yet, notwithstanding all this, I am as certain of going to heaven as if I were there already.

Why, why is all this certainty? Because God, by His Spirit, declares, "Whosoever believeth in the Lord Jesus Christ shall not perish, but have everlasting life." I take God at His word, in childlike simplicity, and hence I have the enjoyment of His promise.

And although I am but a poor, miserable sinner, deserving punishment, yet I know I shall have everlasting life through Christ, and not only shall have everlasting life, but I have it even now. Therefore I have made my calling and election sure.

Moreover, I know by the grace of God that I am not a stony-ground hearer. Why do I know this? Because, having heard the Word I received it, and the cares of this world have not choked it; the persecutions of this world have not dried it up; in the hour of temptation I still bad the word of God in my heart, and did not take my eye away from the cross; and therefore I know I am

NOT A STONY-GROUND HEARER.

I am not a hearer only, but a doer, in some little measure, of the Word; and though I am weak, I can say that I know I have made my calling and election sure. If, after all this, my beloved brethren, you are not sure of it, oh, be not satisfied till the matter is settled.

And what is the result of all this? The beggarly elements of this world affect me very little, because I have heavenly joy in my heart. I do not care for the money, the rank, or the honour of this evil world, and all its other allurements which attract many. I have something better—better far. The heavenly things are the best lever to lift your minds out of this world into heaven. Therefore aim after this certainty as to heaven, and it will raise you above the things of this life.

It is deeply important, my beloved younger brethren and sisters, to make a good beginning in this way, and to continue thus, and then your joy and assurance will increase more and more. Your path will be as that of the just, which "shineth more and more unto the perfect day." Why should it not be so? We ought to increase. You and I are neither prophets nor apostles, yet our path ought, as that of the just, to "shine more and more unto the perfect day."

DILIGENCE

In order that it may be thus, let us give heed to this, "Wherefore, the rather, brethren, give diligence" (mark that word "diligence") "to make your calling and election sure." Why so? "For if ye do these things, ye shall never fall." If you go on in this way, the world will not be able to say, "Look at the drunkard, who calls himself a Christian! Look at that thief who calls himself a Christian! or that idle, slothful man, see how he behaves to his wife; or see how she neglects her family and husband, and yet calls herself a Christian woman."

None shall be able to say such things of the child of God, so long as he continues to walk in these ways of which I have been speaking; and thus reproach shall not be brought upon the name of the Lord, and "if ye do these things, you shall never fall." And you shall never bring dishonour, but rather honour and glory to God.

AN ABUNDANT ENTRANCE

"For so an entrance shall be ministered unto you abundantly into the everlasting kingdom of our Lord and Saviour Jesus Christ." We shall be like vessels under full sail, entering the port. That is what we should aim after, "an abundant entrance." Not like a house on fire, from which there is the possibility of bringing out perhaps a chair or a table, snatched, as it were, from the fire; "a brand plucked from the burning."

In this way some children of God escape at the last content if they simply get into heaven and no more. But this ought not to be the case with you and me. We should be like vessels in full sail entering the port, having an abundant entrance. Let us aim after this, calmly and quietly bidding adieu to this evil world, joyously waiting for the coming of the Lord, rejoicing in the Lord abundantly.

After this we must also aim, so to live as that we may

not have to look back in deep sorrow that we have loved the world. Let us keep this before us, and especially you, my beloved younger brethren and sisters in Christ, while the middle-aged and the aged ought to remember it too; that you have but one brief life to spend for God, and surely this one brief life ought to be spent to the honour, and praise, and glory of God.

I have one more passage, full of deeply important matter to which I wish to direct your attention, by the help of God. You will find it in Eph. 6, and this, for the present, will be the last portion to which I shall direct your attention, except the Lord on Friday evening should lead me to anything else. I shall now only enter upon it, and shall not be able to finish it to-night; but will continue it on Friday evening.

The portion is verses 10 to 18 of chapter 6. This passage, for the first four or five years after my conversion, was one from which, when I came to read it, there was a kind of shrinking in my mind; because I read it merely as a commandment, and found myself reproved by it; therefore I shrank from it.

One Lord's-day, about forty-five years ago, I awoke early in the morning, about five o'clock. I felt tired—very tired, having had a great deal to do on the day previous. I felt I should like to spend another hour in bed; but it came to my mind, "This is the Lord's-day, and there can be nothing better than to rise and give myself to prayer and meditation." I did so, and in the course of my reading I came to this sixth chapter of Ephesians. I began reading; I soon saw that it was full of the gospel —blessedly full of the gospel. It pleased God to bless it greatly to my soul that day, and, ever since, this portion has been particularly dear to my heart.

I desire now, as God may help me, to bring before you what the Holy Ghost would teach us in these verses.

"Finally," the apostle says, as if he meant, Now, after all I have said, let us sum it up in the following verses: My brethren." This word "brethren" is to be especially noticed. As if he meant to say, this is a word for believers, and *specially* for them. "Be strong in the Lord, and in the power of His might."

TRUE STRENGTH

The first point here is, for the beloved fellow-disciples never for a moment to suppose that they have, or can have, any strength of their own. And, because they are converted, and are not now dead in trespasses and sins, and have been brought from death unto life, yet they are not to suppose that they have any strength of their own. "Be strong in the Lord." In ourselves we are utterly weak, and in ourselves we remain weak as we are by nature. Our strength is in the Lord; and by looking to God, through the Lord Jesus Christ, we receive wisdom, strength, help, and, in short, everything we can possibly need as we pass through this vale of tears.

Therefore do we especially need this exhortation, "Be strong in the Lord." We cannot fight, we can do nothing of ourselves; we have no might nor strength of our own. And if any one should say he thinks he has any strength or power in himself, I would say, "My brother, you are mistaken; you have no such thing."

And this we have to remember to the very last moment of our life. I desire day by day, and hour by hour, to remember this, and I request all of you to remember it, that you may never suppose you have any strength or wisdom of your own. If you do so, you are neglecting the resources laid up in Jesus Christ; and moreover if you do so, you will not make use of the wisdom, power, and strength which God has laid up for us in the hour of our weakness, in the person of His beloved Son, the Lord Jesus Christ. Therefore is this exhortation much needed, "Be strong in the Lord, and in the power of His might," "Put on the whole armour of God, that ye may he able to stand against the wiles of the devil."

The next time we shall see, if the Lord will, the deep importance of this exhortation to put on the *whole* armour of God. But now I wish you to notice that it is of great moment that we should

PUT ON THE WHOLE ARMOUR OF GOD.

Not simply the breastplate; not simply the helmet; not simply taking the shield; but the *whole* armour of God. And these words, "put on" the whole armour, are to indicate to us, to make use of the armour. It is to be "put on." It is one thing to know the armour which God has provided. We may know all about it very intimately, but it is a different thing to put it on. Yet, God has provided this armour, in order that we may put it on, and thus be able to stand against the wiles of the devil.

If we do not put it on, then it will profit us nothing. Just as it is with the gospel. God provides it for us; He has made this provision in order that we may escape punishment; and Christ says that they who believe shall not perish, but have everlasting life. Yet if poor sinners do not receive Christ, if they reject Him, and go on trusting in self, or living in carelessness and utter indifference as to the things of God, then all this blessed provision for them, through the sufferings and work of the Lord Jesus Christ, will profit them nothing. They must appropriate it, by God's grace, to themselves.

Now, it is precisely so with the saints. They will not profit by the armour, unless they put it on. But one says, "I am so weak." What then? You stand all the more in need of it; cry, "Oh, my Father, I am Thy weak child; help me to put on Thy armour." God will accept thy cry, and He will help the weak one who so cries.

There is an apparent contradiction between, on the one hand, the sovereignty of God, which is plainly revealed, and on the other hand, the "will of man." We have no power of our own, and yet we are responsible persons. We are commanded distinctly to receive and obey the gospel; and if we do not, yet we are responsible.

If, however, we feel our own utter inability, then let us go to God, and say to Him, "I am weak and sinful, and cannot receive the gospel. Help Thou me." If we do this, we shall be helped, as God is willing to do so, and willing to bless us, if we only seek Him.

So it is with the armour of God. If we are weak, let us say, "Father, see Thy weak child. Yet I wish to put on this armour. Help thou me." You will find that He is willing to help us.

But why is it so important that we put on the whole armour of God, and not a part only? For this very reason, that we should be able to

STAND AGAINST THE WILES OF THE DEVIL.

There are many of those who say, with the ungodly world, that there is no such person as the devil. But the Holy Ghost reveals the fact that there is such a person. I am as thoroughly convinced of this in my inmost soul, as I am convinced of the reality of the person and work of the Lord Jesus Christ; and of the existence of the Father of our Lord Jesus Christ, and of the salvation of all those who believe in the Lord Jesus Christ.

But while it is true that there is such a person, and while it is true that he who is against us is mighty,—very mighty, yet this is also true that He that is for us is still more mighty; and that in the riches of His grace He has created and provided for His poor weak children the whole armour, whereby they may be able to stand against the wiles of the devil. And as long as we make use of this whole armour, we shall find how ready He is to help us in all our weakness and helplessness.

"For we wrestle not against flesh and blood, but against principalities and powers; against the rulers of the darkness of this world; against spiritual wickedness in high places." We have a conflict, but it is not a conflict of this world. It is not according to the ideas of this world. As, for instance, when in an earthly conflict soldier wrestles against soldier, flesh and blood against flesh and blood. Not thus is our warfare. It is of a spiritual character, and altogether against spiritual forces; "against principalities and against powers, against the rulers of the darkness of this world, against spiritual wickedness in high places." In a word, against the power of the evil one.

Here we stop, and from this, if God will, we shall go on next Friday evening to consider the whole armour of God. And those who come here, I affectionately advise to consider it before you come. Read the passage, and seek to meditate upon it with reference to your own heart, and try to see how far you understand these verses.

Thus our meditations, when we come together, will be all the more profitable. I have it particularly laid on my heart to say a word on this portion of Scripture, which I have found repeatedly to be food to my own soul, and which I trust may be also made profitable to others.

COUNSELS TO CONVERTS
IV

The portion from which I have it laid on my heart to speak a few words of counsel and advice, especially to the younger brethren and sisters in Christ, you will find in Eph. 6. 10-18.

I have already observed the deep importance of never, in the last degree, relying on our own power and energy, or upon our past experience, or upon what we think we can accomplish in the things of God; but rather throughout to distrust ourselves, even to the very close of our earthly pilgrimage, and only to rely upon the power and wisdom of God Himself, so that in His power and might we may go forward in the battle.

WE MUST PUT ON THE WHOLE ARMOUR OF GOD;

and regarding this, we have observed the deep importance of putting on the *whole* armour of God. Every part of the armour which God Himself has been pleased to provide for His children, is absolutely required, in order that we may be fully furnished for the conflict. And for this very purpose has the armour been provided, that we may be able to stand against the wiles of the devil. That adversary is very subtle and crafty, and he is ever watching that he may get an advantage over us. In order to lay still greater stress on this, the apostle, by the guidance of the Holy Ghost, proceeds to say, "For we wrestle not against flesh and blood." The battle is not that of army against army, or man against man, as in this world, "but against principalities, against powers, against the rulers of the darkness of this world, against spiritual wickedness in high places."

Here I observe particularly, the deep importance of ever keeping before us, that we have really and truly to fight against the powers of darkness. And if at any time any of us should, through the subtlety of Satan, yield to the temptation that there is no such thing as a real personal devil, let them he aware that that is just one of his chief devices, in order to throw the child of God off his guard, so that he may the more easily get power over him.

THE CAPTAIN OF OUR SALVATION

Verily, there is such a being as the devil. And he is mighty, as well as experienced. But also, for our comfort, let us keep this before us, that greater is He that is for us than all that can be against us. And therefore with courage we may go forth against the powers of darkness and spiritual wickedness in high places. As long as we recognize our own weakness and impotency, and depend upon God, we shall be helped even against these powers.

Thus far we have already proceeded. Now,

"WHEREFORE TAKE UNTO YOU."

Wherefore; that is to say, because the conflict is what it is, and because it is what has been described, because we do not fight against man, or against flesh and blood, but against the powers of darkness, and against spiritual evil powers, "Take unto you the whole armour of God, that ye may be able to withstand in the evil day, and having done all, to stand." For this very purpose the armour is provided for us, that we may be able to withstand and finally to overcome.

Now let not any dear child of God suppose, as there is at times a danger of supposing, that because the conflict is what it is—because it is spiritual, and because our enemies are so many and so mighty, that, therefore, it is utterly useless to attempt to fight against the powers of darkness. Not so. Let us go with good courage to the conflict. The will of the Lord is that we should

"BE OF GOOD COURAGE";

and under whatever circumstances of danger, perplexity, or of trial, the child of God may be placed, let him always be of " good courage." Who shall harm us, if God is for us? If He is on our side, who shall then withstand us?

But let us never trust in self, else we shall quickly find how weak we are. Especially let us never begin to reason with the devil; he is too much for us. The will of God is, never, never, never, under any circumstance, to reason with the tempter. He who begins to reason, is certain to fall; because we have ever to keep before us who the devil is, and what power he has; and, therefore, if we begin to reason, we are sure to be overcome.

THAT OLD SERPENT WHICH IS THE DEVIL

We know not how long the chief of the evil spirits has been in existence; but we know that he was in existence at the creation of the world, and was the originator of evil. Therefore, from the time he deceived our first parents, he has reasoned with a great number of people, and has thus gained a vast experience. Think of all this vast experience, and of all the wiles he has learned, and you will see how absurd it is to attempt to reason with Satan. God's blessed Word is enough, and that is the only thing he cannot stand against. But if you begin to reason with the devil, it is certain that you cannot stand.

Never, then, attempt to reason; especially you, my younger brethren and sisters in Christ. Learn at the outset of the divine life that you must not reason, and that, if you do, you will fall. When tempted, take the blessed book, and say, "My Lord says so-and-so, and I believe it;" and in child-like simplicity rest upon it. Satan cannot stand against that.

"Take unto you the whole armour of God, that ye may be able to withstand in the evil day, and having done all to stand."

Notice further that word

"EVIL DAY."

"What is particularly meant is the day of temptation; that is the evil day. And on that day we are to take comfort in the knowledge that God is our helper. But in a certain sense the whole of this life is an evil day, because of the power of Satan, and because of the world which surrounds us. The devil is ever on the watch to get at us, and therefore in a certain sense the whole time we are in the body is the evil day. The whole armour of God is given to us, not to be used on this particular day, or that, but to be worn during the whole pilgrimage of this life. We may have fought very successfully for a time, but still we are to keep it on.

In the armies of this world, you all know how it is—battle after battle has been fought, and success has been gained. What then? The armour is put off and now, the soldiers rest. But not thus with the armour of God. The whole pilgrimage is a time of war; the conflict ceases not, but must be maintained throughout life.

THE SLEEP OF DEATH

But to you who are not alive spiritually, who are dead in trespasses and sins and have no conflict, I say, affectionately, it is the slumber of death which is upon you. The life which you now live will be terminated, unless you are awakened, in eternal spiritual death. Therefore if you are not awakened, seek with all earnestness of purpose to be made to know your own state, and to seek to become alive through Jesus Christ.

The gospel is yet preached to you—the door of mercy is still open wide. The very fact that you are here to-day shows, that the gospel door is open yet. Oh, press into the door—believe the gospel—obey the commandment to receive the gospel, and trust in the Lord Jesus Christ, and in Him alone, for the salvation of your souls!

Then, if you do so, you will, in the riches of God's grace, receive the forgiveness of your sins; you will be regenerated, and, although you were dead in trespasses and sins, you will instantaneously be made a child of God, an heir of God, joint-heir with Christ; be brought on the road to heaven, and have the bright and blessed prospect of everlasting life before you. Then, and only then, you will know something practically and experimentally of the conflict against the powers of darkness.

It is to those, then, who are believers, and who know what the conflict is, that I speak this evening. And to you beloved brethren and sisters in Christ, but especially the younger brethren and sisters, I say, never allow yourselves to be at ease with regard to the conflict.

It is written here,

"AND HAVING DONE ALL TO STAND."

Oh, how deeply important it is to notice that we must be prepared to stand firm. Again and again do we see the child of God who has set out well, and who has continued for a time to run well, and who has given up the world, with its habits and customs, its passions and pursuits; has renounced all these, and has rejoiced the heart of the Lord Jesus Christ, as well as the hearts of God's dear children; has gone on for a year or two, and then he begins to hanker after this world; then he begins to take his ease in the conflict; another year or two, and he is as much in the world as ever he was.

What a sad, sad, sad case is this; yet how frequently do we see it occur. To avoid it, if I may he permitted to use my experience, I say to the beloved children of God, Be satisfied with nothing short of this, that you are going on in the self-same decided way for God as you did at the beginning. Continue to keep on the armour of God, and say, By His grace I will stand.

Let it never be said of you, That man began well, and has not gone on well. Let it be so that any who knew us in 1830, and now sees us in 1875, can say of us, Well, after forty-five years have passed away, that man is as decided as ever.

I ask myself, and answer it as before God, and I ask you, my brethren also, to answer before God, How is it with us? Are you as decided as at the beginning? If not, there is something wrong. Having been very decided for God is not enough; we must be so still, even continually; ever resisting the powers of darkness and spiritual wickedness in high places.

Let us, then, never settle down at ease to enjoy the victory. That is never the case in this world. There is no permanent victory here; it is far off in yonder world, in the bright blessed eternity which is awaiting us. We shall have victory and rest there, but here, in this life, we have to fight—fight on in the conflict of life.

Now let us consider the armour itself.

"HAVING YOUR LOINS GIRT ABOUT WITH TRUTH"

To most of you, my dear Christian friends, I scarcely need to say, that we have here to keep before us, not the common English soldier with his firearms and modern equipment, but soldiers as they were in those early days, and especially the Roman soldiers. The nature of their armour and warfare we have to keep before us.

Now at that time it was a matter of great importance to the soldiers to have a girdle to gird themselves. By means of this girdle the soldier braced himself for the march and the conflict. The clothes were thus tied close to the body, in order that the soldier might not be hindered in his marching, nor in his fighting, as the fighting often consisted in one man fighting against another man.

Now, in the spiritual conflict, what have we for a

girdle? It is the truth of God. This brings before us the fact, that, just in the measure in which we hold the blessed truths of God's word, so in measure, and only so in measure, are we ready for the conflict.

Every particle of error hinders us in our spiritual conflict. We are helped in the measure in which we adhere to the truth of God. And while the temptation in the case of the young disciple may be to say, "I know I am a child of God, and that Jesus Christ has saved me, therefore what does it matter whether I understand this or that particular truth or not, or this or that particular doctrine or not," yet it is a matter of great moment. Because, in such a degree as we understand the truth, so shall we be able to stand in the hour of conflict, and so much the less shall we be hindered in this our conflict.

We ought to hold the truth in all its parts—every particle of the truth as revealed to us; and we ought not to have our favourite parts, and only those of God's word to which we pay particular attention, to the neglect of other equally important parts. And just in proportion as we seek to know the whole revealed truth, so shall we be strengthened, as with a girdle, for the conflict.

THE BREASTPLATE OF RIGHTEOUSNESS

This part of the armour of a Roman soldier was generally made of a piece of iron or brass, and which particularly covered and protected the vital parts, such as the heart, lungs, and liver. A very important thing, then, was the "breast plate," or piece of iron or brass, covering, as it did, the vital parts of the Roman soldier. Now, we have to ask ourselves, in connection with this, What is this? What have we for a breast-plate to protect us?

One or another says, we must live a righteous life. True, we have to seek to live a righteous life; but this is not the point here. It is this, that we seek continually, as poor weak sinners, to hide ourselves in the righteousness of the Lord Jesus Christ.

In this spiritual conflict there is nothing so important, as that from the very beginning of the spiritual course, we begin as poor miserable sinners, trusting alone in the righteousness of Christ, — the righteousness which the Blessed One has wrought out for sinners, the righteousness in which alone we trust before God. This the only ground on which we expect God to help us, to answer our prayers, and deliver us from the difficulties with which we meet in our spiritual conflict.

THE RIGHTEOUSNESS OF CHRIST

It is, then, deeply important to see that we are poor sinners, miserable and weak in ourselves, but that Jesus is our all and in all; not only thus at the beginning, but thus we must go on; not only two or three years, not even five, ten, or twenty years, and then trust in our own merits, but that we continue as long as we live to depend solely on the righteousness of Christ. It is not only at our conversion that this is so deeply important, when we are made new creatures and enter upon this warfare; but it is equally important at all times in our spiritual life. So that when the devil says—as he will say—"Do you expect to get to heaven, you miserable sinner? You do not deserve it; look at what you have done! No such thing; you need not expect it, you will not get there." When he says that, what is the answer to be? "It is true that I have sinned; yet for Christ Jesus' sake—poor miserable sinner as I am—in His righteousness, I shall yet be in heaven." What is the result of this? You rise!

The devil seems to have you down, and seeks to give you your death blow; yet you rise! He seems to have obtained the mastery over you, and yet you rise again, because you trust in the Lord Jesus Christ and not in self, and you stand before God not in yourself, but in Christ.

And though a poor miserable sinner, yet through Jesus, who makes you clean in His blood, you know you will get to heaven at last.

When you thus go to Christ, and take refuge in His righteousness, the devil is outwitted. Therefore remember particularly to have on this breastplate.

If the Roman soldier had not put on his breastplate how easily he would have been cut down when his breast was unprotected. So it is with us; it is important that we should put on "the breastplate of righteousness."

"YOUR FEET SHOD WITH THE PREPARATION OF THE GOSPEL OF PEACE."

What is the meaning of this? I invited you last Tuesday evening, to meditate on these verses; you may have considered it, but now consider it again with me. What is the meaning of this—"your feet shod with the preparation of the gospel of peace"?

These soldiers, of whom we have been speaking, did not go bare-footed into the battle; for if so, and it were man wrestling against man, how easily they might slip and fall down while fighting one against the other. Neither did they wear sandals, which would not have afforded full protection to the feet. The common thing amongst these soldiers was to wear strong boots.

Many of my friends may remember the name of one of the Roman emperors, Caligula, which means, "little boot." He was called thus because he became a soldier when very young, and his feet were so small that none of the ordinary soldiers' boots would suit him, and he had to have little boots made on purpose for him. I simply remind you of this to show that the common practice amongst the soldiers was, to wear boots, in order that they might be the better helped with regard to their warfare.

Boots also were of especial importance, on account of

marching. The roads at that time were rough and rugged, and thus these boots were of great service in the war, as they had to march, in rank against the enemy. And so our spiritual boots protect us when on the rough march of life, as also in the hour of conflict. We, who are the children of God, have a provision made for us in this respect, and it is the gospel of peace which God has provided for us, that we may be able to march homewards through the rough paths of life, and even to stand in the hour of conflict.

What is this preparation of the gospel of peace? It means, we are the children of God, and we are no longer at enmity with God, but are at peace with Him. Our sins are forgiven in the Lord Jesus Christ. God is well pleased with us for Christ, His dear Son's sake; and we, having no longer any fear, are, at peace with God.

That is the preparation of the gospel of peace, with regard to our spiritual conflict and also with regard to our homeward march. Hold it fast; although thou art a poor, miserable sinner, yet thou art forgiven for Christ's sake, "Through whom we have the forgiveness of sins, according to the riches of His grace." Though I am a poor miserable sinner, yet the heart of the Father loves me, and I am on the road to heaven, where I shall certainly be at last.

Let the child of God hold fast this hope, and this persuasion of his security, as given in the simple statement of the gospel, and by this he will be able to pursue his march heavenwards, and in the hour of conflict he will be able to stand manfully.

All this by having the preparation of the gospel of peace! How deeply important, then, to have clear views of God's gospel, and that we should receive it simply as the gospel, and not in any way mix it up with our own doings or experience. Some would seem to act as if they are to do what they can, and, what they cannot, the Lord will do. Far be it from us to have such thoughts. He and He alone must do all for us. By His atoning death on the cross, He has borne the punishment due to us for our sins, sins which deserved punishment—and nothing but punishment— and has brought us to this blessed hope and trust that all our sins are forgiven; that God is well pleased with us for Christ's sake, and that, sinners though we are, yet He now delights in us for His dear Son's sake, and He is willing to help us in all our conflicts for Christ's sake. Thus we experience that joy and peace, which will help us on the march to heaven, and in the hour of spiritual conflict. So then let us make much of this preparation of the gospel of peace, which is spiritually the protection of our feet, even as the old Roman soldiers were protected by their strong boots.

"ABOVE ALL, TAKING THE SHIELD OF FAITH, wherewith ye shall he able to quench all the fiery darts of the wicked." As the words stand hero in our translation, one or the other might suppose that those words "above all" indicate that it is of the *first* importance to have this shield of faith. Now I do not at all undervalue this shield of faith, but only to point out that this "above all" does not mean that it is of more importance than the other parts of the armour. The meaning of it is, "in addition to all;" that is, not leaving it out.

We have already observed the importance of faith, but this again brings before us the deep importance of exercising faith; and this not only on this particular point, or on the other particular point, but our faith should be exercised on the whole revealed truth of God. In regard to all that He has said as to this world, or the world to come, as well as the first point, that of believing on His dear Son, whom He hath sent into the world. We have to aim after this, that we should increasingly and truly, and with child-like simplicity, seek to take God at His Word. That is exercising faith, which is here called the "shield of faith."

Now in the case of the Roman soldiers, it was deeply important to be protected by the shield. You all know how important this shield was to ward off dangers, such as arrows and blows of the sword. But it was also of great service in warding off darts. So in the spiritual conflict this shield of faith is given, that the child of God should be able to stand against the fiery darts of the wicked—that is the wicked one—the darts of Satan.

"FIERY DARTS"

They are called fiery darts, because they are so painful and so pernicious. We all know, in our own experience, the exceedingly painful nature of these fiery darts, and the only way to overcome them is by using the shield of faith. Exceedingly great temptations are often met with, which tend to make us distrust the love and power of our Father; and the only means of meeting these is by faith. The best way to illustrate the meaning of faith, as applied to these temptations, is just to give one or two instances.

For instance, here is a child of God: suppose that he has been regenerated, and for some time has fought manfully against the evil one, and the allurements of this world. But after a time, perhaps two or three years, he begins to be less watchful. What then? He goes back again, and begins to love this present world, and soon the temptation comes. "Well, I am afraid I shall not be successful, and after all I shall lose the battle." You all know that a child of God may thus be tempted, and how wretched he will be, till he uses the shield of faith to quench this fiery dart of doubt and mistrust. How shall we use the shield of faith? It is stated regarding the children of God, "I will never leave thee nor forsake thee." This is true regarding all the children of God; and it is true regarding you. How quickly, when this is used with child-like simplicity, does it quench that fiery dart.

Or in the temptation which sometimes comes to the child of God, when he is tempted to think that he may, after all, be lost; how does the word of God suit this? Simply by believing what it declares, "None shall be able to pluck them out of My Father's hand." I am one of His sheep, and therefore I cannot he lost. How this will quench the fiery darts of the devil, and give us joy instead of sorrow!

TEMPORAL TRIALS

Now one or two points regarding temporal matters, where faith is also of deep importance. Suppose one who has all his life earned his bread by toil. He gets on towards sixty, and presently will be past it. Now Satan begins to trouble him, and says, "You are getting old now; soon there will be nothing remaining for you but the union or the workhouse."

How wretched and miserable a child of God is made by this; but by using the shield of faith he will be able to quench it. "If my Father has cared for me when young, surely He will continue to care for me when old, and when sick, even as in the past. Or as He says in the Word, 'I will never leave thee nor forsake thee.'" How quickly this temptation will be quenched. I have seen many of God's dear children who were thus troubled.

AN ILLUSTRATION

One instance I remember distinctly, although it occurred many years ago. It was that of an aged widow, a child of God, who had lived very consistently. She had worked hard with her hands in youth, and now in her old age she began to say, I shall have to go to the workhouse. She had some money which she had saved of her past earnings, and she said, "When this is gone I can earn no more, and I shall have to go to the union." I sought to comfort her; I reminded her how God had cared for her in the past, and how He had promised never to leave her nor forsake her; and that as surely as she was a child of God, so surely would He care for her; and that even some of His own children would be led to assist her.

But still the temptation continued, and what was the end of it? Her joy was marred completely for years; she was in deep trouble, simply by this one thought. Yet see how it came to pass at last. One by one the sovereigns were used, and at length it came to the last sovereign; one shilling of it was spent, when the Lord took her to Himself, and there was for her no such thing as the workhouse.

But see how she was losing her spiritual joy, and how her life and her communion with God were marred by this one fiery dart; whereas, if the shield of faith had been used, the devil would have been confounded, and her last days would have been in peace. Therefore, let us use this shield of faith, with the revelation God has been pleased to make of Himself, and we shall soon see the fiery darts of the devil quenched, and have joy.

"AND TAKE THE HELMET OF SALVATION."

In the parallel passage in 1 Thessalonians 5:8, it is, "for an helmet, the hope of salvation." So we have to understand it here, it is the hope of our salvation that is to be our helmet.

All these parts of the armour were of great importance to the Roman soldier; the girdle to bind, the breastplate to defend the vital parts, the boots to protect the feet, and enable them to march firmly, the shield to ward off blows; but although he had all these, there was yet wanting one thing—the iron helmet. Without it, how soon would his head, the most exposed and most tender part of his body, have been injured or hurt. Therefore, the Roman soldier was also protected in this part; his head was protected by the iron helmet.

Thus with the child of God; he has protection for his spiritually weak parts, and it is just this — the hope of salvation. While on earth, we go toiling amidst difficulties, and trials, and temptations. Often all things seem to be against us, and not only the world, but sometimes even the children of God turn their backs on us, and we are left alone, comparatively speaking. Yet, in the midst of it all, there is something unspeakably comforting in this, that makes the heart joyous. What is it? It is "the hope of salvation," the joy of looking forward, and knowing that we shall be in heaven at last.

It is this that keeps us up. The way at times may be very dark, but then it is always a pilgrimage, which is day by day getting shorter as I get nearer home. The journey is ever towards home — nearer, nearer home. It is this bright, blessed prospect of home, home, home — of complete deliverance from sin and temptation, through the blood of Christ Jesus, which strengtheneth us at such times.

To know that we shall be delivered from the old evil nature, to be brought into a state in which the will of God is carried out by us continually, that the mind of God shall be found in us, and that we shall be with the Lord Jesus Christ, who is now at the right hand of God, and shall be like Him—these are some of the bright, blessed prospects of the state to which we are going.

Therefore, my beloved brethren and sisters, especially the younger ones, when temptation, trial, or difficulty come, and when all seems going against us here, remember that this is not our home, and that we must not expect to enjoy this present evil world. Then think of the Father's house, where there are many mansions, and the bright, blessed, and glorious prospect we have of that Father's home, and you will find there is not a better lever to lift us above this world than just to contemplate heaven. Oh, make much of it! make much of it!

For fifty years I have known the Lord, and as grey hairs multiply, and as, little by little, I get nearer and nearer, the prospect becomes brighter and brighter; and during many years of sore conflict, trial, and affliction, this has cheered me exceedingly: "I shall soon be home—soon be with my

Lord." Therefore, make much of this hope, that, even as the helmet protected the Roman soldier, so the hope of salvation may protect you by the way.

Now the last part of the armour:

> "AND THE SWORD OF THE SPIRIT, WHICH IS THE WORD OF GOD."

All the other parts to which we have referred, were in order to protect us from assaults; that is, of a defensive character. Now, here is something to make an attack with—a weapon of an offensive character, with which to march against the enemy, and to make inroads on the powers of darkness.

Not only as the children of God are we to know our weakness, we are also to know and to act as those who have God on our side, One who is both able and willing to help us in time of need; and we should go right among the enemies, that we may pluck brands out of the fire, to the praise, and honour, and glory of God.

Beloved fellow Christians, it is the will of the Lord, that we should not only defend ourselves, but that we should also resolutely seek to win souls, and rescue poor sinners from the snares of the devil, and bring them to the Lord Jesus Christ. For both of these ends there is nothing like the weapon used by our Saviour Himself when tempted, "It is written"; that is, the use of the word of God.

And in order that we may be able to use it to good purpose, we must study it, as I observed last week, regularly and prayerfully, with meditation, and with simple faith, and with self-application. Do not let us reason, but learn ever to take God at His word with child-like simplicity; and when occasion arises bring it out against the devil. Then he will not be able to stand.

This word, the word of God is also to be used that we may win souls for Christ; and not only with reference to them, but with reference to our fellow-disciples, that we may strengthen their hands, and encourage their hearts against the powers of darkness. We can never make too much of the word of God, which must be in our hands as a sharp sword, "piercing even to the dividing asunder of soul and spirit." It is the spiritual sword for the spiritual conflict.

"PRAYING AND WATCHING."

Lastly "Praying always, with all prayer and supplication in the spirit, and watching thereunto with all perseverance and supplication for all saints; and for me, that utterance may be given unto me, that I may open my mouth boldly, to make known the mystery of the gospel."

It is not necessary to dwell on this last part, as I have spoken on it again and again. Only this will I observe, that while all the other points which have been referred to are deeply important, yet they will not he successful unless they are coupled with prayer, constant and believing prayer; for if we should attend to all the other things, and put on the whole armour which God has provided for us, and yet not pray, we shall find how weak and helpless we are.

Why is this? Though we are the children of God we are in ourselves weak, and God will have us to recognise our helplessness in regard to Himself. Therefore, as opportunity and time allow, let us give ourselves to prayer. It is most important to have stated times for prayer, and not to leave it to certain impressions. If we leave it to feelings, you will find that you will be less and less inclined to prayer, and soon will be altogether without it; or, in other words, a poor miserable sinner, without help in the conflict. Have certain times for secret closet prayer, when by ourselves we pour out our souls before God.

In connection with this, let us, as heads of families, have regular family prayer, so that God shall be recognised in the family. As children of God we should also seek to meet with other children of God in prayer, such as prayer meetings. We ought to seek more and more opportunities of fellowship in prayer, as, for instance, in the daily prayer meeting in connection with this hall, where we have met day by day to spread out our wants before Him, and to seek His blessing on our united efforts for the Lord.

Now, my dear fellow believers, attend to these matters which we have been considering, putting on the whole armour of God, accompanied by prayer, and certain I am that you will be happy Christians, holy Christians, and useful Christians. That is what I would desire with regard to all my beloved brethren and sisters in Christ, that they all should be happy Christians; and that they cannot be, except they seek to act according to the mind of God. But acting thus, they will be holy children, and if they walk in His ways and walk with Him, they will also be useful children, as they will be living witnesses for God.

Not only so, but let them aim after being fruitful, bearing fruit thirty, forty, or fifty-fold, and, it may be, sixty-fold. Having attained to this, be not satisfied, but aim after sixty-five, or seventy-fold, and then it might be, and there is no reason that it should not be, a hundred-fold.

May God help us so to live as to bring praise, honour, and glory to His name while life is continued to us.

COUNSELS TO CONVERTS
V

I WISH, my beloved Christian friends, to direct your attention to two passages in connection with prayer. The first you will find in the commencement of Psalm 96, "I love the Lord, because He hath heard my voice and my supplications. Because He hath inclined His ear unto me, therefore will I call upon Him as long as I live."

MARKING ANSWERS TO PRAYER

The Psalmist states, that he loves Jehovah, because He hath heard his voice and his supplications. Now this cannot be the case with us, except we mark the hand of God, and except we observe that He hath heard our supplications, and that he hath answered our prayers. The Psalmist had marked the hand of God, and he says, "I love Jehovah, because He hath heard my voice."

Very few of God's dear children are aware how much this marking of the hand of God with regard to answers to prayer, has to do with increased love to their heavenly Father. We are so apt to leave unnoticed the hand of God, and to pass over what God has been pleased to do in answer to our prayer.

I would particularly advise all, but especially the younger believers, to use a little book, in which they may note down on the one side the requests which they bring before God. There are certain matters which God has laid on our hearts, and we should note them down. It would be helpful to us to write, At such-and-such a time I began to pray for such-and-such a thing; and then to continue to pray with regard to this matter. If we do so, we shall find that sooner or later the prayer will be answered; and then let us mark on the opposite side, that it has, at such a time, pleased God to answer that prayer.

REVIEWING ANSWERED PRAYERS

After some time, read over the memorandum book, and you will find how again and again it has pleased God to answer your prayers; and perhaps regarding matters about which you little expected the answer to come; and soon you will find the wondrous effect of this on your heart, in increasing your love and gratitude to our heavenly Father. The more careful you are in marking what you ask, and what God has given, the more distinctly you will be able to trace how again and again it pleased God to answer your prayers, and more, you will be drawn out to God in love and gratitude. You will find precisely as the Psalmist found it when he says, "I love the Lord, because He hath heard my voice and my Supplications."

THE EFFECTS OF THUS REVIEWING ANSWERED PRAYERS

We ought to love God, even though we have not answers to our prayers; but all this will greatly increase our love; and it is not only once, but if we mark the hand of God, we shall soon find that we have scores and hundreds of answers to prayer. And thus we shall be led to love Him more and more for all he has done. And as we mark how we have been helped, and how gracious and bountiful our Father has been, and how He takes pleasure in listening to the supplications of His children; the heart will be filled increasingly with love and gratitude to Him.

Another effect of all this on the Psalmist we find in the second verse, "Because He hath inclined His ear unto me, therefore will I call upon Him as long as I live." The more evidence we have of His power, and of His willingness to help us, the more our hearts should be determined to call upon the Lord. The more our prayers have been answered, the more should we be stirred up with new determination to ask yet greater things. We should be encouraged to come again and again, in order that He may incline His ear unto us.

Is this, my beloved friends, the case with us? Are those two points found in us, and can we say with the Psalmist, "I love *Jehovah*, because He hath heard my voice and my supplications?" And do our hearts say, "because He hath inclined His ear unto me, therefore will I call upon Him as long as I live?" Verily it should be so with us, if we are believers.

FREEDOM FROM ANXIETY

The second passage to which I desire to direct your attention you will find in the epistle to the Philippians, the fourth chapter, and in the sixth and seventh verses, "Be careful for nothing; but in everything by prayer and supplication, with thanksgiving, let your requests be made known into God. And the peace of God, which passeth understanding, shall keep your hearts and minds through Christ Jesus."

"Be careful for nothing." This by no means signifies that we may be careless, thoughtless, or unconcerned about everything. That is not the meaning of it. The meaning is, not to be anxious about anything. This is one of the privileges of the children of God, that they are permitted, and not only permitted but invited, and not only invited, but commanded, to bring all their cares, sorrows, trials, and wants to their heavenly Father. To roll all their burdens upon God; to cast all their cares upon Him.

And because they are permitted, yea, commanded so to do, they have no need to be anxious about anything. However many or varied our difficulties or necessities, we should commit them all in believing prayer to God; but we should not be anxious. And why not? Because it is impossible to be anxious without dishonouring God.

If the men of the world see that we Christians are anxious like themselves, they will have ground for saying, that our profession of having an Almighty Friend and Helper in heaven is only a profession; and, therefore, we dishonour God by not trusting in Him in the hour of need.

WE HAVE, HOWEVER, SUCH A FRIEND, and He is willing and able to help us and to deliver us in His own time and way. This is the very reason we need not be anxious about anything.

But you say, how am I, a wife with a husband given to drinking, not be anxious? No, I say, my sister in Christ, you are to pray for your husband; you are to pray for that husband very earnestly. But remember to look out for an answer to your prayer; and it is the will of our heavenly Father that you are not to be anxious even in such circumstances. You are earnestly seeking that he should be converted, that is right and proper; but still, be not anxious even in such circumstances. If you roll the burden upon God, and cast all your care upon Him, you will be free from, anxiety even regarding this.

And thus with every matter; regarding our children, for instance, who are unconverted, we have to be careful to train them in the fear of God, to set a holy, godly example before them, to pray much for them, and, at suitable times, to bring the truth before them; but even regarding them, we are not to be anxious. We are to roll the burden—the whole burden—upon God, and He will carry the burden for us.

So—literally—this is to be taken, Be anxious about nothing. And thus we shall walk in holy confidence. Trust in your heavenly Father, looking to Him, confiding in Him, knowing that He will help in His own time and way.

But, while the commandment is not to be anxious about anything, at the same time, we are exhorted to bring everything before God. It is not to make us careless, but to teach us to

LEAN UPON HIM ALONE.

"We are here exhorted to bring the matter before God. "In everything, by prayer and supplication, with thanksgiving, let your requests be made known unto God." Notice especially the word "everything." It is not simply great matters we are to bring before God, not simply small things, but "everything." Therefore, all our affairs—temporal or spiritual—let us bring them before God. And this for the simple reason, that life is made up of little things. If we attempt to stand in our own strength under little trials, we shall find them too heavy for us, and we shall fall, which is dishonouring to God.

THE FOLLY OF NEGLECTING THIS INJUNCTION

Let me see a Christian man who attempts to carry the little burdens in his own strength, and I know that he will soon dishonour God. For we have not a particle of strength to carry any burdens, little or great; and, therefore, we must bring them all to God. And if we attempt to carry them, we shall find that they will increase in weight.

To speak, after the manner of men, God puts a pound weight of trial upon us, and if we take it up and lay it on the shoulders of our heavenly Father, it is gone; but if, on the other hand, we attempt to carry it ourselves, what is the result? Soon it will increase to ten pounds, and if we still try to carry it, it will increase to a hundred-weight, and if we try still to stagger under it in our own strength, it will increase still more, in order to lead us to cast it upon God.

Now our wisdom is just this, when we have any little burdens, let us tell our heavenly Father, "I have no strength for this weight, I cannot carry the burden." Well, our heavenly Father is ready to do this for us; He has commanded us to roll all our cares on Him, and not to attempt to carry them in our own strength. Let us then cast all our cares and "burdens upon God, and He will carry them for us.

"SUPPLICATION."

Therefore it is so deeply important "in everything, by prayer and supplication, to let your requests be made known to God." With prayer; and not only with prayer, but with supplication; that is, with earnestness and with entreaty, just as the beggars sometimes act. They ask for alms; well, you seem not to listen and pass on, but they go after you; perhaps twenty steps, and sometimes even a hundred yards or more. They follow you, still asking, until they obtain the alms they desire.

Now this is what we have to do; not simply to mention our request before God, but to go on asking again and again, with earnest prayer and supplication, until we receive. Just ask as a beggar would do; and will not our heavenly Father give it to us, seeing that He hath bestowed His greatest gift, even His Son upon us?

"THANKSGIVING."

Again, we have specially to notice that prayer and supplication is coupled with thanksgiving. That is, if I may say so, that we should lay the foundation in the way of thanksgiving, and upon that, place the superstructure of prayer and supplication. We should praise the Lord for what He has given us already; while asking Him for more blessing.

We are frequently very remiss in this; we forget to render praise for the mercies already received from our heavenly Father. This should not be so.

THE CERTAIN EFFECT OF ALL THIS

In the next verse we have the precious result of all this, "The peace of God," what a precious result of such a way of acting is this; our hearts are at peace, instead of hurrying hither and thither, as men beside themselves, and instead of great excitement. Instead of all this, the result of prayer and praise will be our hearts will be at peace.

We shall have the peace which passeth all understanding. And that peaceful calm which is so precious, and which no words can describe, and which is called "the peace of God" shall be in our hearts. "The peace of God, which passeth understanding, shall keep your hearts and minds through Christ Jesus."

"KEEP YOUR HEARTS."

The idea of a garrison, is in that word "keep." And the meaning is that our hearts shall be kept by the peace of God, as by an occupying garrison.

There is much in these verses; and whilst the men of this world, and even some children of God who know not these truths, and do not ask thus, are wretched, and anxious, and hurrying about like people beside themselves, when trouble or excitement come; we, the children of God, who know these precious truths, are able calmly to wait on the Lord, and to leave ourselves quietly in the hands of God. Thus the peace which passeth understanding will rule in our hearts arid minds, and we shall not merely find help, but we shall be kept from false ways, and bring honour to God before the world, and shall thus comfort greatly the children of God, to the praise and honour and glory of His name.

COUNSELS TO CONVERTS
VI

As the Lord may help us, we will meditate this afternoon on a few verses in the third chapter of the Lamentations of Jeremiah, from the 22nd verse: "It is of the Lord's mercies that we are not consumed, because His compassions fail not." (Read on to the close of verse 26.)

On these verses we will meditate this afternoon. I never undertake, according to my own judgment, to choose a subject for meditation. When I have the prospect of preaching, I wait on God, and ask Him to direct me to a subject. So I have asked Him repeatedly for a portion for this afternoon, and this is the portion to which I felt directed. And now, may the Lord grant us a blessing!

We have particularly, in the first place, to consider the circumstances under which Jeremiah wrote these words, "It is of the Lord's (Jehovah's) mercies we are not consumed." We have to consider the state in which, as a nation, the Israelites then were.

THE CONSEQUENCES OF SIN

Almost all the Jews had fallen victims either to the war, or to famine, or to pestilence, or had been carried away as captives to Babylon. Only the poorest persons were left in the land, and even these were in very small numbers. In order that the whole land might not be desolate, the king of Babylon gave orders that a few men should he left behind.

Further, Jerusalem was burned and destroyed. The walls had been broken down round about the city, and the Temple was burned. Under these circumstances the prophet says, "It is of the Lord's mercies that we are not consumed, because His compassions fail not." He meant to say, if we had what we deserve, we should be utterly destroyed. Not a single man would be left alive; not a single house in the country but it would be destroyed. And if any should be left, they deserve no longer to be taken up by Jehovah. That is what we deserve on account of our sins. The prophet finds that all this has come upon them in consequence of their sin.

Now, in order to make this practical to ourselves, let us ask, If we had what we deserve, what would it be? We could expect nothing but entire destruction. If we were treated in the way of justice and judgment, and not according to mercy and grace, what could there be but destruction for us?

I ask you to put the question each one to himself with regard to this: Have I been convinced that I am a sinner—and such a sinner as to deserve punishment, nothing but punishment? If you have never been convinced of this—that you are a sinner, and that, as a sinner, you deserve nothing but punishment, then I ask you affectionately to consider it now; and to consider the only ground of salvation, and whether you have yet seen that your punishment has been laid on the Lord Jesus Christ. And if you are thus a sinner, and deserving of punishment (whether you see it or not, it is a fact, revealed by the Holy Ghost), then consider that God, in mercy, that you might not be punished, has sent Christ, His only-begotten Son, to bear the punishment in our room and stead, as our Substitute.

God, in the riches of His grace did that, in order that we might escape the punishment and destruction due to us, which punishment must have been visited on us, unless He had done this. Therefore was the Lord Jesus visited with stripes, and it was that which nailed Him to the accursed tree, in order that He might bear the punishment, and that we might be saved, eternally saved; that we might be happy, eternally happy.

Now do we all see this? And if not, I ask you, prayerfully to read the first three chapters of the Epistle to the Romans. There it is plainly stated, what we are by nature and what we merit. And if you do see this truth, then I especially ask you to entreat God to help you to believe on the Lord Jesus Christ; for thus, and thus alone, you can escape the punishment. If you trust in Him, you shall not be punished; for through Him do we obtain mercy, even "the forgiveness of sins, according to the riches of His grace;" and if we believe, we become the children of God; "and if children, then heirs, heirs of God, and joint heirs with Christ." Through believing the gospel, we are "delivered from the power of darkness, and translated into the kingdom of God's dear Son." And thus there is before us the bright and blessed prospect of eternal joy and happiness, through the Lord Jesus Christ.

SELF-ABASEMENT

Notice particularly also here, that the prophet does not say, it as of the Lord's mercies that these wicked Jews are not consumed, but "that *we* are not consumed." In this he includes himself. This is particularly to be noticed, for Jeremiah was one of the holiest men then living; and yet he includes himself when he says, it is of Jehovah's mercies that we are not consumed—that *I* among them am not consumed.

So it is with those that fear God, and are believers in the Messiah; whether believing in the Messiah which was to come, as in Jeremiah's days, or as now, in looking back to the Messiah as having come. The more they know of God, the more they see their own corrupt nature, their own sinfulness and shortcomings. And, instead of having a proud, haughty spirit towards fellow sinners, we include ourselves with them, and say, with the prophet, "it is of the Lord's mercies that we are not consumed."

The heart of God was still towards the descendants of Abraham; the compassionate heart of Jehovah was still towards the literal seed of Abraham, and the blessings which had been promised to that seed were not forgotten; so that the prophet could say, "new every morning."

This is the language of all who really know God, of all who are acquainted with God, and who have watched His hand in any small degree. Daily do they say that the compassions of Jehovah are indeed new every morning, and that great is His faithfulness. And if it were not thus, what would become of us who have known the Lord Jesus Christ? We should soon fall back, if left to ourselves. We should soon fall into that corrupt state from which we were delivered, if left to ourselves. It is "by God's grace that we ace what we are; just because He is faithful to us. Although we should be unfaithful for a time, yet He abides faithful to His people. How blessed is it to know this!

Again, "Jehovah is my portion, saith my soul; therefore will I hope in Him." This comforted the prophet in the midst of the sorrows which surrounded him. The people were almost all slain by the sword, or had perished by famine or pestilence; and the few who were left were for the most part carried away captive. The city of Jerusalem was destroyed, and the Temple burned.

Very few of us can enter into the full sorrow of the prophet under those circumstances; but this is certain, that it was an immense trial to him, especially the last circumstance, that the Temple was destroyed. Yet mark, he is not overwhelmed; there is yet hope. Hope in what? Hope in the living God: "Jehovah is my portion, therefore will I hope in Him." The living God remains to me. Though the people are destroyed, though Jerusalem is destroyed, and the walls thereof broken down, and though the Temple is burned, yet God is my portion. That is the special point of our meditation—

"JEHOVAH IS MY PORTION."

God was all to him, and that is particularly my message to all my fellow disciples this afternoon. How is it with us regarding this? Is the living God our portion? Do we find Him to be our all? Is the living God our portion and our hope? Remember, whatever else we have, He must be our portion. Suppose for a moment that all our friends turned their backs on us, yet if God Himself be ours, how rich are we? If we were possessed of much wealth and property, and were to lose it all, yet with God Himself as our portion, we should be rich. And if we were to spend the remainder of our lives in a dungeon, yet if God remains with us and goes with us there, we can be unspeakably happy. What are all these things if we have God? Have we, my dear friends, Him for our portion? I do not ask you now, are you religious people? I suppose you are, because you are here to-day. I do not ask if you read the Bible; I suppose that yon do. I do not ask if you go to a place of worship; I suppose that. I do not ask if you bow and then pray; I suppose you do. I do not ask if you give a little money to the cause of God; I suppose that. But, I ask more than all this, far, far more than all this, Do you find in God Himself your all? I ask you nothing short of this, that you ask yourself now, as before God: Is my wife my portion? Is my husband my portion? If so, then a poor portion you have. It is right to have natural affection towards your wife or your husband. It is right and proper for parents to love their children, and for children to love their parents; otherwise it would be sinful in the highest degree. But, none of these relatives are to be our portion as the children of God; Jehovah Himself must be that. He would have us satisfied with nothing short of Himself. I ask you whether this is the case with you? With some, the treasures of this world are their portion—what a poor miserable portion! You will find such are unhappy, and have guilty consciences. You will never be satisfied by the treasures of this world—never.

But others make their business their portion. They are very earnest in attending to their business. Quite right in its place this. I do not wish at all to encourage idleness in any way in reference to this; for Christians should attend carefully and attentively to their business; if they do not, they will not have God's blessing on their business. But yet, if the business is our portion, if money-making, or rank, or standing in life, or anything in this world be our portion, or what we seek to find satisfaction in, then I say it is a poor, miserable portion, by whatever name it may be called. But if, on the contrary, we have God for our portion, if in Him we seek to find satisfaction, and in nothing else, then have we a rich portion indeed. Is He only our joy, our hope, our happiness? Are our hearts in Him? our hopes in Him? our everything in Him? Have we all this? Let us be honest before God. Let us be honest with ourselves. Have we *one* thing we care about, and is that God Himself? Or, have we two things, or ten things that we care about? There is *one* thing only that should be uppermost in our hearts, and that is God Himself; *one* thing that should be our portion, and that is God Himself. The prophet Jeremiah had this portion, and therefore could never be miserable, poor, or forsaken. All is right so long as the living God Himself is our portion. As was the case with the Lord Jesus Christ Himself when on this earth, He had only one object, and that was, to live for, and serve God, His Father, to do His work. "My meat is to do the will of Him that sent me." And so it should be with us, that everything we do should be done for the praise, and honour, and glory of God. This should be our ruling motive. All our thoughts should be occupied with God, either directly or indirectly; even our coming together to meet our friends should be with reference to God—even our eating and drinking should he with reference to Him. Do we seek strength to live and labour for God, and do we spend the strength for Him, which we may have obtained?

Let us then ask ourselves the question,

"IS GOD HIMSELF MY PORTION?"

I do not ask you, without asking myself the question, What is my portion, my happiness, my *all?* Is it God Himself, or the things of this world? I answer for myself, I could not be satisfied with anything short of this, that God, and God alone, should be my portion, day by day, and week by week, month by month, and year by year. Oh, beloved friends, stop short of nothing till you come to this, that God Himself is your only portion. The consequence of having Him for your portion will be, that whatever be the circumstance in which you are placed, whether there be war, or famine, or pestilence, or whatever be the circumstances connected with your present life, still you can be happy in the midst of them all. Let it be sickness, or danger, or even the prospect of. death itself, God is yours, and you will yet be happy; but if God Himself be not your portion, you are dependent on, and affected by circumstances, and you will be more or less miserable in accordance with the things which surround you. But if you can say "Jehovah is my portion," you can look forward to brighter and happier days. Jeremiah had this hope, and he looked forward expecting that the people would be brought back again, that Jerusalem, would be built again, and that the Temple would be restored. And so it was, after about seventy years. Because the promises were from the living God Himself to the descendants of Abraham, therefore he could say, "The Lord is my portion, therefore will I hope in Him."

But people will say, this was very well in the days of the prophets and the apostles, but now, in the latter part of the nineteenth century, we cannot expect such things. I believe no such thing. Why should not the people of God be as happy in their God, as ever the prophets or apostles were? Why not? Is not He the same God? Is His power not the same ? Is His love to His children not as great as ever it was ? Is His willingness to help His children not as great as ever it was? Certainly it is. The blessed Book remains with us; the precious promises are still there; and therefore we ought to remember, that to trust completely in the Lord, and to be happy in Him, is yet as possible as it was to the children of God in the middle of the first, or the beginning of the second century. Why not? There is nothing at all to hinder. You and I are certainly not apostles or prophets, but the blessing of peace, and joy in the Holy Ghost, and of the blessed promises, we may enjoy now in the nineteenth century as much as these believers of old; and, together with the prophet, we may say, "Jehovah is my portion, saith my soul; therefore will I hope in Him."

Again, "The Lord is good unto them that wait for Him." What an especial encouragement this is with regard to the trials and difficulties of life. All of us have sooner or later to pass through, difficulties and trials, our path is not always smooth. Yet, in these circumstances, let us lay hold on such a word as this, "Jehovah is good unto them that wait for Him." To all that wait for Him, He is very good. Let us go and make known our requests to Him, and seek His help, and wait till it comes. For the promise is, "Jehovah is good unto them that wait for Him." There is something to be had by waiting on the Lord. He is good to them that seek Him. This is especial encouragement to any who may he here who know not the Lord, who are not yet believers in Him. Here is the promise: "The Lord is good to the soul that seeketh Him." What they have to do is, just to ask God to have mercy upon them. And they will find that He is good to the soul that seeketh Him. To any inquiring about the things of God, I would say, the soul that seeks Him will have blessing.

And especially is this comforting to us, the believers in the Lord Jesus Christ. "Whatever our trials, perplexities, and difficulties, there is the promise, "The Lord is good to them that wait for Him, to the soul that seeketh Him." There is no such thing as seeking God in vain; the seeking soul shall find. He will not seek blessing, comfort, instruction, power over natural evil tendencies from the Lord in vain. Whether we seek power over our temper, or pride, or high-mindedness, or wilfulness, or whatever may be in us, contrary to the mind of God, let us just bring the case with childlike simplicity before the Lord, and we shall find that it is not in vain to seek the Lord, but that "He is good to them that wait for Him, to the soul that seeketh Him."

Now we come to the last verse upon which we will meditate at present. "It is good that a man should both hope and quietly wait for the salvation of the Lord."

HOPING AND WAITING

In the first place, "It is good that a man should hope for the salvation of Jehovah." Regarding the word salvation here, it is to be understood as it is generally used in the Old Testament, not merely deliverance from sin and punishment, as it is generally used in the New Testament, but in the wider sense of the word, deliverance generally. Thus it does not here mean only deliverance for the soul—though that is not excluded—but it means deliverance generally from trial, temptation, sorrow and difficulty. For this salvation or deliverance, it is good for us to hope in the Lord. All of us at times find ourselves under circumstances from which we need deliverance; then it is good to hope for salvation from Jehovah. Are we doing so? It is the will of the Lord regarding us. It is here stated, that it is good to do so and you will find it is good—practically and experimentally you will find it to be good in your own soul. The devil's aim, when trial and affliction come, is to whisper to your heart—"Ah, this may last for ever!" "I shall never get out of this." You are looking forward anticipating a life-long burden. Listen to Jesus, "Sufficient unto the day is the evil thereof." Leave everything in the hands of God. Aim at being in such a position, that you can look to Him, and seek from Him, grace for the present day; and He will give it. As for to-morrow, if it comes, the Lord will give grace for it also.

Remember, when the thought comes into your mind, "I shall never get rid of this;" that it is good for a man to hope for the salvation of Jehovah; He will deliver. Trial and affliction will come; well, never mind, deliverance will also come, for the Lord is good. If you do not hold fast this hope, if you lose it, and give up the comfort that God would bestow upon your soul, then you will find yourself losing the comfort and strength you would otherwise have. Therefore I say, hold it fast.

Remember the memorable passage in Psalm 27:13, where David says, "I had fainted, unless I had believed to see the goodness of the Lord in the land of the living." All my strength would be completely taken away, except I were expecting to see better days. That is what we have to do, to be looking out for brighter and happier days, more blessed and cheerful days, which the Lord will send if we wait for Him. That is the thought which comes from the Spirit of God; the other thought, that of hopelessness, comes from the evil one, in order that, if possible, he may make us wretched, and that we should give up hoping in God, and should sit down in despair, as if no good were possible. But "it is good that a man should hope for the salvation of Jehovah." And this is not all; it is said, moreover, it is good that he should *quietly* wait for the salvation of Jehovah. Thus, we have not only to hope, but we have to wait, and wait quietly. This you and I cannot naturally do. We want to have our deliverance at once; we would have it to-day, and do not want to wait, or that it should be delayed. And if it does not come when we want it, the temptation is to think ourselves wiser than God, to begin to complain, to be dissatisfied, and even to begin to murmur, because it is so. Now, all this is dishonouring to God, and should not be. The will of God is, that we should make known our requests to Him; in the meantime leave ourselves in His hand. And, for our comfort, remember the words, "All things work together for good to them that love God." This should sustain us in the meantime, together with the hope that He will finally deliver us. And if this deliverance is not yet, then our business is, quietly to wait, and by quietly waiting, to honour God; because then it will be known to those who see us, that we have a Father in heaven, a Father who cares for us; and that we are watched over and cared for; and that we trust and rely upon the Father in the assurance that "all things work together for good for them that love God." Let us seek to carry away a blessing.

THE CONCLUSION OF THE MATTER

First of all, then, let us remember that, whatever trials or afflictions befall us, it is nothing at all to what we deserve. We all deserve eternal punishment, even hell. Therefore let us say with the prophet, "It is of the Lord's mercies that we are not consumed, because His compassions fail not. They are new every morning,"

The next point is, that Jehovah Himself is our portion and our hope. Let us be satisfied with nothing short of this, that God Himself is our all.

The third point which I desire you specially to carry away is, that when trials and afflictions come, as come they will, we remember that "it is good to hope and to wait for the salvation of Jehovah;" and not only that we begin to wait, but that we go on quietly waiting till the deliverance comes. And then it becomes us to bless and praise God for what He has done.

THE GOD OF JESHURUN

FOR our meditation this evening I have been directed, after prayer, to a few verses in Deut. 33:26-29. "There is none like unto the God of Jeshurun, who rideth upon the heavens in thy help, and His excellency on the sky." (Read to the close of the chapter.)

This portion, as most of you know well, is connected with the blessing which Moses gave to the various tribes of Israel, just before the Lord took him away. After giving a particular blessing to each one of the tribes, the blessing in these verses is now uttered, by the Spirit speaking through the prophet, with regard to all the tribes of Israel—with regard to the whole of the literal Israel. The Holy Ghost sums up all the previous blessings in this last, which He begins by the words, "There is none like unto the God of Jeshurun."

IMPUTED RIGHTEOUSNESS

Jeshurun means, "the righteous," or "the righteous one." And this is one of the titles given to the Israelites. Strange title, is it not? to be given by the Spirit to that stiff-necked people, who had again and again provoked the God of Israel, and who had sinned against Him times without number. Stiff-necked and rebellious though they had been, yet they are here called "the righteous." In speaking of this people, the Holy One calls them "righteous."

Precisely so is it with ourselves—by nature we are sinners, and great sinners; and not only so, but deserving punishment, and nothing but punishment; yet the moment a poor sinner is brought to believe on the Lord Jesus Christ he is called righteous. "We are all by nature children of wrath, even as others," yet by faith in the Lord Jesus Christ we are accepted, regenerated—that is, born again; instead of the children of wrath, we become the children of God, we are brought out of darkness into His marvellous light, are delivered from the powers of darkness, and translated into the kingdom of His dear Son" —are brought on the road to heaven, and have before us the bright and blessed prospect of our Father's house.

SAVED BY GRACE THROUGH FAITH

Through faith in the Lord Jesus Christ, these and all other blessings of the gospel become ours. Fear is lost, judgment is taken away, and instead of all that, we instantaneously become children of God. And this may be obtained by all sinners here present. There are such, in all probability, here at this moment, who are still in the bonds of unrighteousness, who are going on their way in spiritual darkness—who belong to the kingdom of darkness—who are dead in trespasses and sins.

To such I have to say, instantaneously you may obtain the forgiveness of your sins, be made alive in Christ Jesus, and be "delivered from the powers of darkness, and translated into the kingdom of His dear Son;" but this is alone to be obtained by faith in the Lord Jesus Christ.

OH, GLORIOUS GOSPEL!

that we should be called the sons of God! When I think of myself, and when other believers think of themselves, when we look inward, we see that we are utterly unworthy of such honour—we can indeed see anything but righteousness. Yet we are called "righteous."

If this title was applied to these oft-provoking and stiff-necked Israelites—if they were called "Jeshurun"— the righteous ones, how much more abundantly is this applicable to those who are united to the Lord Jesus Christ, and who partake by faith of His perfect righteousness?

Now, regarding these Israelites, it is here stated that

"There is none like unto the God of Jeshurun." There is no god like unto their God. They had the living God, while others had but dead idols.

THE LORD OUR PORTION

And this is especially our portion: we have the God and Father of our Lord Jesus Christ to be our God and Father. That is, we have the living God on our side, to be our God, our Guide, our Father, and our Friend. All this, however, is only true of us if we believe in the Lord Jesus Christ. We may speak about Him as our God; we may read about Him; we may be able to explain certain passages of Scripture concerning Him; we may even have written much about Him; and may have preached in His name; and yet it may not be true of us that we have the living God for our Father, except we really believe in the Lord Jesus Christ, and trust in Him alone for the salvation of our souls.

But if we do thus accept Jesus as our Saviour, then it is true of us that we have God as our Father, and we have the same precious share in those blessings as the literal Israelites had, and it can be said of us, "There is none like unto the God of Jeshurun."

THE LORD OUR STRENGTH

But further, with regard to these blessed ones, it is said, "Who rideth upon the heavens in thy help, and in His excellency on the sky." Look at this expression, "Rideth upon the heavens in thy help." Such a thought as this would never have entered into the mind of the greatest poet who ever lived, except he had borrowed it from the Bible. All the best and noblest ideas in the poets they have borrowed from that source. The thought here is, that there is none who can resist God—that no power on earth can oppose Him. Pass through all England, France, Germany, or America, and there are none equal to Him. The powers of this earth—that is, all under heaven—are as nothing before

Him. He is the Creator—they are the creatures, and they cannot withstand Him, who is above all.

THE LORD OUR DELIVERER

Now, the comfort to us is, that we have such a God for our helper—one who rides on the heavens—in the very sky; we have Him to fight on our behalf. He is above all, He is out of the reach of Satan and wicked men, He cannot be opposed by any of them. He is above the elements, and they cannot withstand Him, neither can any creature stand against Him, who is the chiefest of all. He is on our side, He is for us, and if He be for us who can be against us? If He is on our tide all is well with us. But, alas! if He is against us, what shall become of us? If we are in Him we are in perfect safety.

But if there be anyone here who has not God on his side, who has never believed on the Lord Jesus Christ, let me exhort you, yea, even implore you, be you reconciled—be you at peace with God. If so, then you will be safe, and then it will be said with regard to you, that "He rideth upon the heavens in your help." All that we have to do, feeling as we must our own weakness, impotency, and helplessness, is but to cast ourselves into His arms, and say, "My Father, I am Thy child, Thy poor, weak, helpless child; be nigh unto Thy child, and help him."

What will our Father, who rides upon the heavens, do? Most assuredly, He will assist His poor weak child. Whatever his necessities may be, he may feel assured that the everlasting arms are around him, and that His Father will thrust out the enemies, and will destroy them utterly.

TRYING CIRCUMSTANCES

Remember, that when this blessing was given, the Israelites had not yet entered the promised land, although on the point of doing so. Moreover, even if they had crossed the Jordan, there were still the seven mighty nations of the Canaanites to be overcome; and therefore at such a time they needed the help of the living God, and were blessed by being reminded that they had such a helper.

And so with us, the Israel of God, and the heirs of the promise. We have much conflict yet before us, and so these words are for our encouragement. God, the living God, is our refuge. As if the Holy Ghost by the prophet would say, "True, you have these great and mighty enemies to overcome, but in going forward, remember that God will he at your side as your helper. Commit yourselves to Him, look to Him, trust in Him, depend on Him, and you will find the power of His mighty arm will save you." What He would have us remember and take courage in, is the fact, that

THE ETERNAL GOD IS OUR REFUGE.

Can we, each one of us, say this, "God, the eternal, living God, is my refuge"? For myself, I can say He is my only refuge, and has been so for fifty years. How many of you can say the same? Ask yourselves individually this deeply important question. If you are able to say this with regard to yourselves, what a happy people you are. But if not able to say it, yet there is no reason why you should not he able to say it. It is only trust in Him that is required; nothing else but to place yourselves wholly in His hands. This blessing is ready for us, but waiting to he received and appropriated. It is for "Whosoever will," as in that precious hymn we have just been singing—

> "Whosoever will—the promise is secure,
> Whosoever will, for ever must endure;
> Whosoever will, 'tis life for evermore,
> Whosoever will, may come."

There is nothing to hinder anyone who is here present having it now, if he will. If you will only depend on the Lord Jesus Christ for the salvation of your souls, it may be yours now. Just as it is true of me, a poor, miserable sinner, and true of many thousands who, like me, a poor miserable sinners, but who now trust in Him, so it may be true of you, that there is none like *your* God, who rideth upon the heaven in your help.

"THE ETERNAL GOD."

But further, "the eternal God is thy refuge, and underneath are the everlasting arms." There is something peculiarly sweet to me in this verse; it tells me that I have an eternal Friend, a living Friend, a Friend who is above all, who has all power and might, and that He is on my side.

It is well indeed to have an earthly friend, who, if yon are in poverty, may help you. But sickness may come, he may be taken away by death; or, if not that, he may lose all his wealth with which he helped you, and thus may be unable further to assist you. But none of these things affect the living God—He is the same yesterday, to-day, and for ever. Eternal is thy refuge. Fifty years ago He was as now; a thousand years ago—ten thousand years ago—He is ever the same.

The God of Elijah is here to-day, and He is exactly the same as He was in the prophet's time—as ready and as willing to help His children. The living God is with us, whose power never fails, whose arm never grows weary, whose wisdom is infinite, and whose power is unchanging. Therefore to-day, to-morrow, and next month, as long as life is continued, He will be our helper and friend. Still more, even as He is through all time, so will He be through all eternity. Oh, the blessedness of having the eternal God on our side! Not only on our side, but on whom we may rely as on a fortress of strength, in whom we may get refuge continually, and in whom there is perfect security.

FALSE VIEWS OF CHRISTIANITY

If the world only knew the blessedness of thus having

God as our refuge, I think the whole world would seek at once after the Lord. It is only because they think it is something miserable to be a Christian, and do not know that it is infinitely more precious to be a Christian than to be without God, that they are content to remain unsaved.

This is one great reason why they do not seek to enjoy the things of God. And it is just the reason why you and I should make it our business to be out-and-out Christians, that we may show to the world what it is to be truly happy Christians, and at the same time be living examples to the Church. But this true and real joy cannot be possessed unless we are out-and-out Christians. There must not be a seeking to hold fast the things of the world to the utmost, and yet seeking to get to heaven all the same. If this be the case with us, we shall just have enough religion to make us miserable, and too little to make us happy.

WHAT DOES GOD WANT?

That we should be happy Christians; and this we can only be if we are holy Christians. We shall never, of course, be altogether free from sin on this earth; not that until we are taken home. But we must aim after being holy children; we must not go on in what we know is contrary to the divine will. And if we are really out-and-out Christians, and are really holding on to the eternal living God, the result will be that we shall be happy Christians, and shall be bearing testimony to those "that are without."

And the result of this will be to stir them up to seek after the Lord; and so a thousand Christians will be a. thousand witnesses for the living God. Therefore, my beloved brethren and sisters, let us lay it to heart to be out-and-out Christians, so that we may lay hold of this word—

"THE LIVING GOD IS THY REFUGE."

I am a weak erring sinner, yet I have the living God on my side, the eternal God as my refuge. Oh, the blessedness of having such a refuge as this. What are all earthly honours in comparison with this? What the highest dignities? What the greatest earthly crown as compared with the blessedness which we possess in having the living, eternal God on our side, and of being permitted to make Him our refuge?

And this is the position of the child of God; above everything that man can conceive, "underneath are the everlasting arms," with the power of the almighty God for our helper. What a comfort in our helplessness, to know that although you and I are weak, erring, and feeble naturally, and can do nothing if left to ourselves; yet we have these everlasting arms underneath us to support us. Though we are helpless, here is an Almighty arm to lean upon, and even to lie upon. It is an arm that can carry us through the difficulties which lie before us, and through the trials which await us; can bear us safely through— can carry us in all our helplessness. Oh, the blessedness of the figure used here—"The eternal God is thy refuge, and underneath are the everlasting arms!"

THE DELIVERER

Further, "And He shall thrust out the enemy from before thee, and shall say, Destroy them." What a blessed promise was this to the Israelites! Before them was the Jordan to be crossed; and even if it were crossed, were there not those great and mighty nations to be overcome? Looking to themselves, they might well have been afraid; but it must not be thus, there must be no fear in those underneath whom are the everlasting arms. Further, to encourage them, Jehovah distinctly says with regard to these seven mighty nations, I will thrust out the enemy from before you, and will say, "Destroy them."

Look at the entrance of the children of Israel, and see how this was fulfilled. Look at the crossing of the Jordan; see how the walls of Jericho fell. Look at the various, battles with the enemy. When the kings came against them, how easily they were overcome. When nations united against them, still Jehovah was on their side; and at last, all were thrust out and destroyed—overcome by the power of Jehovah.

Now, this is particularly comforting with regard to ourselves. We are a feeble band, a "little flock;" our enemies are mighty and strong. "We have no power in ourselves against this great army." So we must look on all this as a hopeless case, and exclaim, "We can never get to heaven; we are so weak, helpless, and sinful in ourselves." Well, it is quite true, we are so weak and helpless in ourselves, that we cannot overcome those that are against us; but our Helper is mighty, and though these enemies were ten thousand times more numerous than they are, and though they would easily overcome us if faced in our own power, yet it is still true that

JEHOVAH SAVES,

and that He has promised to thrust out the enemy from before us, even to destroy them. All the power of evil will not finally prevail, though at times it appears as if it would be so. Neither shall the corrupt nature within us finally have the victory; but through the Lord Jesus Christ we shall have the victory, and be more than conquerors.

Therefore, right blessed is the prospect before us! If we look at ourselves, there is abundant reason to be cast down. Yet we must never forget the word, that we shall have victory through the Lord Jesus Christ, for "greater is He that is for us than all that can be against us," and through the God and Father of our Lord Jesus Christ we shall finally have the victory.

GOD'S DELIVERANCES

In the literal fulfilment of the promise with regard to the Israelites, the enemy was destroyed, but not at all through their own strength. It was solely by God helping them that these were destroyed. Remember how God fought for them, time after time. How the sun stood still at the request of Joshua. How, again, the elements from heaven fought for them; how stones were hailed upon the enemy. The hornets also were by Jehovah used for the destruction of the enemies. In various ways Jehovah fought on their behalf, and showed His mighty power in leading His people to possess the land.

So now with the Israel of God; they can of themselves &o nothing, having nothing but weakness ; but again and again God delivers them; so that while in this life they can never be perfectly delivered from the power of the enemy, yet they shall finally be helped by their God.

Further,

"ISRAEL THEN SHALL DWELL IN SAFETY ALONE."

I wish you to mark this word, "alone," most particularly. It contains the idea of "separation"—safety in separation. "Israel then shall dwell in safety alone." The safety is dependent on their dwelling alone; the safety is dependent on their entire separation from other nations. It was to be their peculiar position of separate-ness from others: it was to be their very safety. God intended them to be separate, He forbade their entering into marriage with the other nations, or in any other way forming connections with them. They must destroy the surrounding nations and walk separately.

Now if my beloved brethren will walk according to the mind of God, that is what they must do—come out, and be separate. There must be separation from the world. Naturally, we are inclined to give up the line of demarcation, and to say, "This is too strict, too particular; why should I be so much separated from, the world? See that brother; he is enjoying the world a little; he is mixing with the world, and so is able to make something of each world, and he is a Christian. Why should not I also be able to mix somewhat with the world, and yet get to heaven at last?"

Mark! mark! my beloved Christian friends. What the Lord requires is, that we should live

SEPARATE FROM THE WORLD.

Of course, as our business is here, we must have something to do with the world, yet we should not go on in the *spirit* of the world. It is quite possible that we should conduct our business carefully, and yet be separate to the Lord. God does not see it good to take us out of the world. Jesus prayed with regard to us, "I pray not that Thou shouldest take them out of the world, but that Thou shouldest keep them from the evil." The Apostle says, "Come out from among them, and be ye separate." Thus, if we desire to attain nearness of communion with God, we must be willing to live in separation from the world, and to aim at a decided line of demarcation between the world and the Church, which will be for the praise, honour, and glory of God. This we cannot do if we are living as the world does, or seeking to be as much like the world as possible, In so doing we shall only bring dishonour upon the name of God, and misery upon ourselves. Beloved Christian friends, let us keep rank against the world, living in separation from its habits, maxims, and principles, and aim at conformity to the mind of the Lord Jesus Christ, rather than, as many seem to do, to try to live as much like the world as possible.

WE OUGHT TO BE A "MARKED PEOPLE."

Men should know that we are servants of the Lord Jesus Christ; even as our blessed Master Himself, who did not seek to be like the scribes and Pharisees, but rather sternly denounced them. He Himself said, that He must be about the business of His Father; that was His grand object. And that is what we must aim after. In the business and matters of this life we must of necessity mix, to a certain extent, with the world, but we must, day by day, and hour by hour, seek to live as much as possible unlike the world. Thus only is it that we bring forth fruit abundantly to the praise, honour, and glory of the Lord.

I would ask you most affectionately, my beloved brethren and sisters, "Are you willing to be such disciples—such out-and-out Christians, and to be such children of God?" This, remember, is the kind of children that God looks for; such disciples the Lord Jesus desires to have—men who are willing to live *only* for Him. Such children, such disciples, are certainly needed for these days, especially in view of the wondrous manner in which God has been visiting the whole of our land within the last twelve months. At such a time the eyes of the world are upon us, to see if we do live according to our profession. Surely, then, it in expected that we should live so that we may bring glory to God.

By thus living out-and-out for the Lord, we should become bolder and bolder. He will grant us more grace and more help, and we shall be delivered, "Thus Israel shall dwell in safety alone." Even so. And "The fountain of Jacob shall be upon a land of corn and wine." That means

FRUITFULNESS—

the fountain in the midst of a land of corn and wine. But in the Hebrew, the word here rendered "fountain" also means "eye," and therefore it means "the eye of Jacob shall be upon a land of corn and wine." The land into which the Israelites were to be brought, was to be a land of plenty, "a land flowing with milk and honey." "When they entered the land, they did find abundance. So with reference to ourselves, having been brought into safety, we shall also be brought into a land of plenty. We shall be fed with the finest of the wheat, and with corn and wine, for strength and for encouragement in the work of the Lord.

"Also the heavens shall drop down dew." We are to be

brought into a fruitful country spiritually, in which there is no such thing as drought. The children of God have the promise that they shall be well watered, their soul shall delight itself in fatness.

"Happy art thou, O Israel; who is like unto thee, O people saved by the Lord, the shield of thy help, and who is the sword of thy excellency! and thine enemies shall be found liars unto thee; and thou shalt tread upon their high places." This was spoken just as they were about to enter the land of promise.

"HAPPY ART THOU, O ISRAEL."

They were, it is true, about to enter the land, but before them they had the great and mighty nations. Now if this was true of the literal Israel, how far more abundantly ought it to be true regarding the Israel of God. Believers in the Lord Jesus Christ, here present, is it true of you and of me? "Happy art thou, O Israel." Can we say positively of each and every one here present, "*thou* art happy," and "*thou* art happy? Can we say this of ourselves? If we cannot, yet we ought to be able to say it. There is no reason why we should not, if we are really believers in the Lord Jesus Christ. It ought to be true, but *is* it true of you all? It might, and ought to be.

I desire to give my testimony that it *is* true of me. Though a poor miserable sinner, I am a very happy man. Though just now nearly seventy years of age, and though having been fifty years in the spiritual life, yet I have not grown unhappy; I am still very happy. Even as it is true of me, so it might be true of each of you. Why not? It is the will of our Lord Jesus Christ, that all His disciples should be happy disciples. Let us, then, aim after it.

Now, in leaving home for the second time to speak as God gives me opportunity, it is my desire to do my little part, in order that the children of God should be happy children of God. For there is such a thing as being holy and happy children—such a thing as being thoroughly decided Christians, and yet being happy. It is the will of the Father that we should be happy. What is the reason that we are not *all* happy? Let each of you ask the question, and answer it before God to yourselves— "Why, why, why am I not a *happy* child of God—a happy disciple of the Lord Jesus Christ?" There is nothing whatever to hinder us, so far as God's truth is concerned. God delights to see you all happy. Do not say, "Oh, Mr. Müller, if you had my trial, my burden, you could not be happy." What a mistake! The Christian may he ever a happy man. "While the world is dependent upon surrounding circumstances for apparent happiness, the Christian may he truly happy, whatever his circumstances may be, so long as he is really trusting in God, and satisfied with Him.

Therefore, my beloved Christian friends,

NEVER ATTEMPT TO CARRY YOUR OWN BURDEN, but learn to roll it upon the Lord. Seek to deal with Him about everything; if you have any trial, any perplexity, cast it upon Him, then you will find out how ready He is to help, and you will be able to say, even in view of all these circumstances, "I am happy."

If we are "unhappy, the fault lies with ourselves. There is no reason why we should not be happy children. Our Father loves us, and He will lead us safely through. Having such a Father, it may well be said of us, "Happy art thou, O Israel; who is like unto thee, O people saved by the Lord, the shield of thy help, and who is the sword of thy excellency."

These Israelites were happy because they had such a God. Look how He delivered them and saved them. It was He who delivered them from the Egyptians, who led them through the Red Sea, destroying the hosts of Pharaoh. It was He who led them through the wilderness, provided them with heavenly food, and water from the rock, and finally led them into the land of promise.

CAUSE FOR HAPPINESS

And remember that it is by Him that you and I are delivered from a worse power than Egypt; are delivered from greater enemies than the host of the Egyptians and by Him we are led through the many difficulties of this life. Daily He is leading us, until at length He will land us safely above. Ought we not then to be happy truly happy in the Lord? I ask you, affectionately, is it so with you? Are you all happy Christians? You ought to be, if you will only look to Him. God bless these words, bringing before us, as they have to-night, that He is willing and able to help us, and willing and able to fight our battles for us, until at last all "thine enemies shall he found liars unto thee; and thou shalt tread upon their high places." So it was with the literal Israel, and so it shall be with us, through the Lord Jesus Christ.

Now, in conclusion, if there be any here present who know not this blessedness, let them seek that this blessing may be theirs, through faith in the Lord Jesus Christ. They may have all these blessings, if they will only trust in Him alone for the salvation of their souls. As for the many hundreds here present who believe in the Lord Jesus Christ, let them remember, that though weak, vile, and erring sinners in ourselves, yet, by the grace of God, we are what we are, and through faith in the Lord Jesus Christ, laying hold of His righteousness, and His strength, we shall have the living God for our helper; and, in the midst of all troubles, we may still he truly happy. He is willing to do for us all we need. Trust Him with child-like simplicity, and you will see how ready He is to help you, and to give blessing.

THE SECRET OF PREVAILING PRAYER

I DESIRE, beloved Christian friends, to bring before you, for encouragement in prayer, a precious, instance in which an answer to united supplication is given, as we have it recorded by the Holy Ghost, in Acts 12.

"Now about that time Herod the king stretched forth his hands to vex certain of the church. And he killed James the brother of John with the sword." This was the first apostle who became a martyr for Christ. Stephen had previously been stoned, but he was not an apostle. This one was an apostle.

SATAN'S POWER LIMITED

"And because be saw it pleased the Jews, he proceeded further to take Peter also." Now Peter, indeed, seems to be at death's gate; but the Lord said, "Thus far shalt thou go, and no farther." This we have to keep before us, that Satan, though he hates us, can go no farther than the Lord gives him liberty.

The most striking instance of this, we find in the case of Job. Satan had tried to get at him but was unable to do so; and at last he has to make confession before Jehovah, "Hast thou not made a hedge about him, and about his house, and about all that he hath on every side? Satan had tried to get at him, but by reason of the hedge he was unable to get at the person or substance of Job. It was only by the permission of Jehovah, and when this hedge was removed, that he was able to get at the substance of Job. And even still, the hedge was around the person of Job, and not until this hedge had been removed, was he able to touch the person of Job. Though we must never lose sight of the fact that on the one hand Satan may be, and often is, powerful to hurt us, yet on the other hand, He that is with us is more powerful still, and Satan can do nothing without the permission of Jehovah.

"And when he had apprehended him, he put him in prison, and delivered him to four quaternions of soldiers to keep him." He was delivered to sixteen soldiers—four little companies of four soldiers each, who were to he responsible for him; so that there might be two inside, and two outside, and so always some to take care of him. Thus it seemed to be utterly impossible that he could escape. "Intending after Easter to bring him forth to the people." It is called Easter here, but there was no such thing as Easter then. It was the feast of unleavened bread.

"Peter, therefore, was kept in prison; but prayer was made without ceasing of the church unto God for him." Here we have prayer in church capacity. The saints at Jerusalem, meeting together, and giving themselves to prayer, and from what we see afterwards, it was

"PRAYER WITHOUT CEASING."

There was always some little band at prayer—"prayer was made without ceasing of the church unto God for him."

They did not say, Now we will send a petition to Herod to let him go. They might have sent in such a petition, for by this time there were thousands in Jerusalem who believed in the Lord Jesus Christ. They were a formidable company by that time; and if they had all written down their names to this petition they might have succeeded. And if thus they did not succeed, they might have raised a large sum of money. They were very willing to give their substance, to sell their houses and lands for the poor of the church; and most certainly they would have willingly done so for the deliverance of Peter. They did not do this, though a most probable way of getting Peter delivered would have been to have bribed some of Herod's courtiers. Even in this very chapter we find that when disunion had arisen in regard to the men of Tyre and Sidon, some individuals bribed a courtier, the king's chamberlain, and thus made peace. Therefore it might possibly have succeeded if they had done so. But none of these things did they use; they gave themselves to prayer. And that, my beloved friends, is the best weapon they could have used. There is not a more blessed and powerful weapon for the children of God, than that they should give themselves to prayer. For thus they can have the power of God on their side—the almighty power of God. And by making use of this power, through the instrumentality of prayer in all things we need, we can have the infinite wisdom of God brought to work for ns, and have God Himself at our side, as children of God. Therefore we should seek to make a far better use than ever we have done of prayer. And you, my beloved Christian friends, who are in the habit of meeting often at the noonday prayer meeting, expect great things at the hands of God; look out for wondrous blessings, and you will find how ready He is to give those things which we ask for. This, then, these saints at Jerusalem did—they gave themselves to prayer without ceasing. That is, they believed that though Herod had apprehended him for the purpose of slaying him, and though this Herod was a notoriously wicked man, as we all know, yet God was able to deliver him from this bloodthirsty Herod. They believed that nothing was too hard for God to accomplish, and therefore they prayed without ceasing.

WAITING FOR THE ANSWER

Now, notice, we do not know how long Peter was in prison, but it is an obvious and natural inference that he had been apprehended before those days of unleavened bread; as after these days his execution was to take place, and, therefore, at least he was in prison seven days. Now, it was not on the first day that the prayer was answered. They met together and prayed,—prayed earnestly; but the first day, hour by hour, passed away, and yet Peter was in prison. The second day, and again they are found waiting on God in prayer. Still, hour by hour, the second day passed, and yet he was not delivered. And so the third, and fourth, and fifth days passed away. They are still waiting on God; prayer is made without ceasing; yet this holy man remained in prison; and there seemed to be no prospect of God answering their prayers.

And thus, beloved friends, you and I shall find again and again that the answer is delayed; and the question is, shall we give up praying, or shall we continue? The temptation is to cease praying, as though we had given up hope, and to say, "It is useless; we have already prayed so long that it is useless to continue." This is just what Satan would have us say; but let us persevere and go on steadily praying, and be assured that God is both able and willing to do it for us; and that it is the very joy and delight of His heart, for Christ's sake, to give to us all things which are for the glory of His name, and our good and profit. If we do so, He will give us our desire. As assuredly as we are the children of God, if we pray perseveringly, and in faith, the prayer will be answered. Thus let us learn from this precious instance regarding prayer, which the Holy Ghost has given for our encouragement.

"And when Herod would have brought him forth, the same night Peter was sleeping between two soldiers, bound with two chains, and the keepers before the door." Mark, that the last night before his execution is now come, and yet Peter is asleep. Not carelessly and indifferently was he lying there, but calmly, quietly resting in the arms of Jesus, and leaning on the bosom of his Lord. He is bound with two chains, as the custom was, between two soldiers, one on the one side and one on the other side, that he might not escape.

GOD'S MANNER OF ANSWERING THE PRAYER

And now about the deliverance; we will see in what way God works.

"And behold, the angel of the Lord came upon him, and a light shined in the prison." We should have said, this must be done in the dark, and as quietly as possible. But see, the light came into the prison. Humanly speaking, this would have wakened the soldiers; but not thus with Jehovah; when He works, He can do His will, notwithstanding all these things.

The angel "smote Peter on the side, and raised him up, saying, Arise up quickly," without any fear that in addressing Peter the soldiers should he wakened.

"And as he rose, the chains fell from off his hands." Still there was no fear of arousing the soldiers.

"Gird thyself." There is no need to hurry; he is to be taken out, but is to dress himself properly.

And now comes the strangest thing of all, "Bind on thy sandals." These wooden shoes must be bound on the feet. We should have said, let him walk out without them, that no noise be made to awaken the sleeping soldiers. Not thus; it was God who wrought the deliverance, and when He works there is no need to fear, for who can withstand?

And so he did. And the angel saith unto him, "Cast thy garment about thee." His outer garment is to be put on. Everything, therefore, is to be done in an orderly manner. It is as if Herod had sent a messenger to deliver him; he is to go quietly forth.

"When they were past the first and second ward." The eyes of the keepers were miraculously shut.

But now they come to "the iron gate." Many, many times do we come to some such iron gate. He was now out of the prison, and past the soldiers who were watching, but now he comes to this great iron gate. How shall he get out of prison after all? And so it is with you and me at times. Everything seems prepared, and difficulties have been removed; and yet, after all, there seems to be one great obstacle which is insurmountable. Can we escape? Yes; God is able to open the iron gate for you and for me, even as He caused the great iron gate of the prison to open of its own accord. Lot us expect everything from God, and He will do it, if it is for His glory, and our good and profit.

THE UNCHANGEABLE POWER OF GOD

But can He do miraculous things in the latter part of the nineteenth century? Yes, as well as He could in the middle of the first century. Let us never say this was in the days of the Apostles, and we cannot expect such things now. Quite true, that God does not commonly work miracles; but He can if He will, and let us give glory to His name, that if He does not work miracles it is because He can and does do His will by ordinary means. He can accomplish His ends in many ways. Let us never lose heart in such circumstances; He has the same power as ever He had. Many think if they were living in the days of Elijah, or in the days of Elisha, or in the days of the Apostles, they would expect these things; but because they do not live in those days, but in the latter part of the nineteenth century, therefore they cannot expect to have such answers to prayer. This is wrong; remember, that God has the same power as in the days of the prophets of old, or of the Apostles of old; therefore let us only look for great blessings, and great blessings will be bestowed on us, my beloved friends in Christ.

"They passed through one street, and forthwith the angel departed from him." This contains an important spiritual truth—it is this, that God does not work miracles when they are not needed. The angel was sent to deliver Peter from prison; but Peter was now in the streets, and he knew very well the streets of Jerusalem. He had been living there, and he knew all about them; and it was not, therefore, necessary that the angel should lead him through the streets, and bring him to the house where he was going. Therefore as soon as he was outside the prison, and no more supernatural help was required, the angel departed from him.

THE DELIVERANCE EFFECTED

"And when Peter was come to himself, he said, Now I know of a surety that the Lord hath sent His angel, and hath delivered me out of the hands of Herod, and from all the expectation of the people of the Jews." He wist not that it was true at first, and thought that it must be a vision, but now that he finds himself in the streets, he knows that God has indeed delivered him.

"And when he had considered the thing, he came to the house of Mary the mother of John, whose surname was Mark, where many were gathered together praying." Notice this, "many were gathered praying." For what purpose? For Peter's deliverance unquestionably; because prayer was made by the church on his behalf without ceasing. Though it was the night before his execution, they did not lose heart. It is to be next day; to the eye of man the case seems hopeless, but they still come together to pray. Therefore they had not only begun well, but they had also gone on well; they had continued in prayer.

"And as Peter knocked at the door of the gate, a damsel came to hearken, named Rhoda." Her name is given. "Why so? When this was written down, inquiry might be made as to the truth of the account. The damsel, probably, was then living, and thus opportunity for this inquiry was afforded. "And when she knew Peter's voice, she opened not the gate for gladness, but ran in and told how Peter stood before the gate."

Here we find a description to the very life. What shall we say? The damsel heard his voice and knew it; she knew they were praying for Peter's deliverance; her heart was so glad that first of all she runs to tell that Peter stood at the door. She could not open the door. Now what do we expect to hear out of the mouths of those beloved brethren in Christ, those holy men who have been waiting upon God day after day? Surely it will be praise. "They said unto her, Thou art mad."

FAILING FAITH

Ah! there it is which shows what we are. "Thou art mad." I specially seek in bringing this before you this morning, that we may learn what we are naturally. They had begun well, and had gone on well, yet failed completely in the end. They had faith at the first, and exercised faith, but had no faith in the end. Let us be warned, beloved friends; that is just what we must seek to avoid. It is comparatively easy for us to begin well and to go on well, day after day, week after week, mouth after month; but it is difficult to remain faithful to the end. Even thus it was, beloved Christian friends, regarding those of whom we are quite ready to say, "we are not worthy to unloose their shoes;" and if they failed, what of us? What say they? "Thou art mad." They are praying for the thing, and it comes; yet this is what they say. Those men had begun in faith, had gone on in. faith, and yet it is gone. They had continued outwardly to wait upon God, but at last without expectation. If they had continued in faith, they would have said, when they heard the tidings, "Blessed be God; let His holy name be praised!" It could not have been otherwise, if they had been waiting to the end for the blessing; and since it was not so, it is a plain proof that faith was gone. I am as certain of this as though an audible voice had told me from heaven. It would have been impossible for them to say to that dear, godly young woman, "Thou art mad," when she brought the news of Peter's deliverance, unless faith had been gone. This, however, is what we say naturally, "Thou art mad."

IF WE ASK LET US BE LOOKING FOR THE ANSWER

"But she constantly affirmed that it was even so. Then said they, It is his angel. But Peter continued knocking; and when they had opened the door, and saw him, they were astonished." Another proof that they were wanting in faith at that time, "they were astonished." True faith is thus known, that when we begin in faith, and continue in faith, we are not astonished when the answer comes. For instance, suppose any of you, my Christian friends, have beloved sons or daughters who are unconverted in America, or in Australia, or in New Zealand, for whom you have been praying long. At last you get a letter, stating that at such-and-such a time they have been brought to the Lord. The test, whether you have been praying in faith or not, is, if say when the letter comes, "The Lord be praised for it," and you receive the tidings gladly; then you have been exercising faith. But if not, if you begin to question whether it is real, can it be the case? Then by this you know you have not been exercising faith; you have not been expecting your request to be granted. If I may use a phrase in the right sense, although one of the world's phrases, the world says of certain things, "We take it as a matter of course." So, in a spiritual sense, we should be so confident that God will bless, and that He will do for us in answer to prayer what we ask, that when it comes, we should still be so confident as to say, like the world, "we take it as a matter of course; it could not be otherwise; the thing must come, because God has pledged Himself, for Christ's sake, to give the blessing."

"But he, beckoning unto them with the hand to hold their peace, declared unto them how the Lord had brought him out of prison. And he said, Go show these things unto James and to the brethren; and he departed, and went into another place."

THE BRIDE OF CHRIST
Canticles 4:12-16, and 5:1

As the Lord may help us, we will meditate this afternoon on the last five verses of the fourth chapter of the Song of Solomon, and the first verse of the fifth chapter. The division into chapters is simply a human arrangement, and it becomes us by no means to read or meditate on the Word of God according to that arrangement, but to observe what the Holy Ghost would teach us: sometimes the very point to be learned being lost by the division made.

THE CHARACTER OF THE BOOK

Most of my dear Christian friends here present, if not all, know very well that in this part of the divine testimony, called the Song of Solomon, or Canticles, we have brought before us the wondrous love of the Lord Jesus Christ to His Church, and the love of the Church to the Lord Jesus Christ, her Redeemer, under the figure of bridegroom and bride.

This is just one of the portions which we should consider as well as any other portion of God's Word. "We may naturally have little inclination for doing so, and the reason is, because our hearts are so little towards His Lord Jesus Christ, and we know so little of this real personal attachment to Him. Yet this is the very reason why we should bestir ourselves to increase in love, and to get into such a state of heart that we may understand something or the Song of Solomon. If our hearts were in greater sympathy with what we find in the Song of Solomon, we should soon see that this is just the state of heart which will find its highest degree in Heaven. And surely we should never rest satisfied till we get in some little degree to understand and enter into the joys of Heaven—till the aspirations, feelings, and desires of Heaven are found m some measure in us now.

THE NAMES GIVEN TO THE CHURCH

Notice first, that the Lord Jesus Christ calls the Church His spouse, His sister. Wondrous grace towards sinners such as we are! When we remember that we are but wicked, guilty, and rebellious sinners by nature, does not His wondrous love indeed amaze us? Such is this love, that while we naturally are so sinful, and while each of us only seeks to gratify himself, yet the Lord Jesus Christ looks upon us as His sister and spouse. Wonderful: yet thus it is!

And this is not only said regarding the eminent saints, as John the aged in Patmos, or Paul the prisoner at Rome. It is said of them; but it is also true of you and me, provided that we trust in the Lord Jesus Christ for the salvation of our souls. Every one of us who accepts the provision which the Lord has made for sin in the person of Christ,—every such an one has scriptural warrant to look upon himself as part of the spouse of the Lord Jesus Christ, and as belonging to the bride of Christ.

THE ABSENT BRIDEGROOM

Oh, how precious, how unspeakably precious and blessed is this! We are His bride, and the Lord Jesus Christ has gone to prepare a place for the bride—a mansion in His Father's house; and when He has made it ready, He will come again to take the bride to Himself. For the Lord Jesus cannot be satisfied, until the Church, His bride, is with Him in the place of honour and glory, which the Father has given to Him as the reward of His perfect obedience—His obedience even, unto death—in this world, while doing the Father's will. "I will come again, and receive you unto Myself, that where I am, there ye may be also."

So, when we read such a portion of Scripture as the one before us, we should read it with reference to ourselves. Each one of us should say, Though I am a poor miserable sinner, I belong to the spouse of Christ; I am part of the bride of the Lamb. Do you say this in your hearts? Who among you can say this? Do all of you, who trust in the Lord Jesus Christ for the salvation of your souls, say of yourselves, Though naturally I am a, vile, wicked sinner, yet I do belong to the bride of Christ, I am one of those for whom He is preparing a place. I shall be with Him in the mansions which He is getting ready. Soon He is coming to take me with Him, that I may be where He is.

You see it is just in the measure in which we are able to appropriate the statements in the Scriptures to ourselves, that we enjoy them. The point is not how much we speak about these things, how much we write about them, how much we read about them, how much we preach about them. It is not how many books we may have written about the things of God; but it is how far do we appropriate them to ourselves, and know the power of them in our own hearts. Only in so far as this is the case, will the Word of God be really profitable to our own souls.

Now here, before going any further, the point is,

DO WE BELONG TO THE SPOUSE OF CHRIST, OR NOT?

If I do believe in Christ, and trust in Him alone for the salvation of my soul, that is the point. Let each of us see if this is the case. Can we each say, Although I am a poor miserable sinner, yet I have trusted and do trust in Him. If I have never seen that I am a sinner, and as a sinner deserving punishment and nothing but punishment, and for escape from this punishment, have never trusted in the Lord Jesus Christ, then all these things do not refer to me. But, while this is the case, it is not too late yet. The door is still open, that we may enter and find mercy. Just as in that beautiful hymn we have just sung—

> "Whosoever cometh need not delay,
> Now the door is open; enter while you may;
> Jesus is the true, the only living Way;
> Whosoever will may come."

Only let us put our trust in the Lord Jesus Christ for the salvation of our souls, and then all these blessings apply as really and truly to each of us as they applied to John in the Isle of Patmos, or to Paul the apostle a prisoner in Rome. Therefore, now—now—now is the time. The door of mercy is open wide still. God is willing to hear for Christ's sake. Come thus, and you will have salvation.

I suppose that those to whom I speak are all in this blessed state; but if not, let them come thus, and they will be brought into it.

Now let us see what the Lord Jesus Christ says of His Church—

"A GARDEN ENCLOSED IS
MY SISTER, MY SPOUSE."

What does this mean? Literally it means, barred—locked up. But what is it intended to convey here? When a garden is locked up, as we all know very well, it is that the proprietor may have the right only to enter, or those to whom he may give this right; and that not every one may have access to the garden to help himself to the fruits as he pleaseth. The garden is not only enclosed by walls, as would seem here; but in the Hebrew it is "locked-up," or "barred;" so that none but the proprietor may have access. Who is He? The Lord Jesus Christ: and He alone may have access to our hearts, and not any one else, as He pleases.

What, then, does this deeply important truth convey to us? Simply that we are bought with a price, even the precious blood of Christ; that we are set apart for the glory of Christ. He, and He alone, has any right to us, and the devil has none.

THE BELIEVER IS NOT HIS OWN

More than this, we have no right to ourselves. "We are not our own, we are bought with a price." We are not our own masters. No one can say, My time is my own, as the world does say. It is not mine. My time, my talents are not mine, they are God's. My business even is not mine, it is God's. My house, my lands, my purse, everything I have is not mine, it belongs to the Lord; for He has bought me with His precious blood, and having bought me, He has purchased all that I have.

All this is implied in the figure used, "a garden enclosed." But, beloved brethren, and sisters in Christ, let me ask you affectionately, Is it thus with you? I have desired, time after time, to press the passages, upon which we have been meditating, home to your hearts; so this afternoon do I desire to impress this point on your hearts. Do you enter into this? Do you rejoice in this, That you are not your own, that you are bought by the precious blood of Christ, and that you and all you have belong entirely to Him? Your hands, your feet are His, and therefore are to be employed for Him. Your eyes, your tongue, your talents, your time, and your purse, are all His, and therefore to be used for Him. Your business and your possessions are His; everything you have belongs to Him, being bought by His precious blood, and thus set apart for His use. He has access to all these things, and He alone ought to have this access. He is the Master, and we are but stewards whom He will order as He pleases.

Let us seek to enter into this, that we are set apart for His use, and so we shall be enabled to bring forth more abundant fruit to the praise and honour and glory of God. This is intended by the Holy Ghost to be conveyed to our hearts by the figure, "a garden enclosed."

But there is still more.

"A SPRING SHUT UP."

Why is it shut up? When an earthly spring is shut up, it is that not everyone may have a right to it, but that the owner, or any to whom he may allow the right and privilege of access to the spring, may be able to drink of the water, and none others.

It is, then, another figure used by the Holy Ghost to teach us the truth we have already been considering—to show us that we are the Lord's, and that we are set apart that He may use us as He pleases. That we have no right to our time and talents, but that they all belong to Him.

Some think it is all the same how they spend their time, whether in learning to play instruments or otherwise. Others have a desire to learn sciences or languages, and they think they have a perfect right to do so if they feel inclined. Now I do not mean to say that such things are sinful, if we have time for them; but no one has any right thus to employ his time or talents until he has laid it before the Lord, and has asked, Is it Thy will that I should spend my time in learning to play this instrument, or this science, or this language? Shall I thereby serve Thee or otherwise? If it is the will of the Lord, then it is right and proper thus to employ our time. So with everything we have, as our time, money and talents, they are His; and we ought not to use them unless it be for the praise and honour and glory of God.

But here another figure is used, not only a garden enclosed," and "a spring shut up," but also

"A FOUNTAIN SEALED."

Further, and more particularly still, not simply "a spring shut up," but still more pointedly, to mark that the owner of the spring alone has right of access to it, it is called "a fountain scaled." It is His, and His only, and therefore there is a seal on it; and no one dare break that seal to take water out of the spring.

The spring is His; the water which is in it came from Him; the water that He has put there is for Him and for His use. Therefore, the living water which is in it, is to be used only for the praise, and honour, and glory of His great name. This brings before us for the third time, more minutely than before, that we are the Lord's. Therefore we are to learn to be more decidedly out and out for the Lord; and we should never look on ourselves as belonging to this world, or as being our own; but should ever remember that we are bought with a price, even the precious blood of Christ, and that thus we, and all we have, and all we are, belong solely to the Master for His glory and use.

JOY OF CHRIST IN HIS CHURCH

So much for the first point in. the portion before us. Now the Lord Jesus Christ speaks in praise of His bride, the Church. And how does He speak of her? "Thy plants are an orchard of pomegranates, with pleasant fruits; camphire, with spikenard; spikenard and saffron, calamus and cinnamon, with all trees of frankincense; myrrh and aloes, with all the chief spices; a fountain of gardens, a well of living waters, and streams from Lebanon." He means by these figures to convey the delight which He, the bridegroom, takes in the Church, His bride; to show us how dear we are to His heart, and what loveliness and beauty He sees in us. And how He is delighted with our service, although it may be but little, and how our worship and praise are sweet as incense to Him. Wonderful, is it not? that such as we poor miserable sinners are, should yet be able with our service, and worship, and love to give delight to the Lord. Everything we do or think is in a greater or less degree mingled with sin, and yet we are acceptable—even delightful—in His sight.

AN ILLUSTRATION

Take, for instance, this poor service I am rendering for Him now. I have set out from home to offer a word here and there, as God may give me openings; and as He may help me, I am seeking to speak a word, specially of counsel and advice, for the younger brethren and sisters in Christ, to uphold the honour and glory of His name. One or another may say, "What a good thing that is! But what does this poor worm say of himself? Before my God, I say I am a poor, miserable sinner. Although I do not live in open sin, and do not give occasion to people to point at me and say, "See what he is doing again; see how inconsistent he is." Not thus with me; but still I am but a sinner in myself, and all I do or say is more or less mixed with sin. All my efforts need the precious blood of Christ to cleanse them; and I have to go with my preaching to the Lord, to make me clean in all these pool attempts to serve Him, or to help my brethren.

ACCEPTED SERVICE

Yet with all this, I know that the Lord Jesus looks on me and on my service with complacency and with delight; and that He delights in me, and that He says of me, "He is my beloved servant: I will go with him as he labours for me, I delight in his work and will accept his service as rendered unto Me, in the riches of My grace." That is the thought of the blessed Lord and Master concerning me, His unworthy servant; while I myself see nothing but defilement in my service.

Such is the truth taught us in these verses—the joy of the Lord in His Church. It is that the Lord Jesus Christ looks with delight and complacency on His people. He does not see sin in us: He sees His own comeliness reflected in us—His own beauty in us, and His own spotless righteousness, and therefore it is that His eye sees in us that which is beautiful, lovely, and which pleases Him. All that is in us good is of Himself and not of us.

This brings before us another deeply important point. It is this: that if the Lord Jesus Christ looks on us with delight, although weak and erring as we are, so we should look on each other. The natural tendency is, to see in our brother or sister their failings and errors; but we ought to aim after this—to find out Christ in one another; and if there be found in such and such a poor sinner anything of Christ, though it be but little, then let us delight in it.

BEARING THE INFIRMITIES OF THE WEAK

There is frequently much weakness at first in the divine life, but spiritual strength will increase. Just as we see in Nicodemus, who at first came to Jesus by night for fear of the Jews; and also in the case of Joseph, of Arimathea, who at first did not own the Lord boldly and plainly; yet afterwards, we find them so much grown in grace, that when all the disciples—courageous Peter and beloved John—had forsaken their Master and fled, then these two, who were so weak at first, came openly forward and asked the body of their Lord, that they might bury it.

Therefore we ought to look lovingly on weak disciples, for they may be strengthened and put us to shame; and you and I, instead of looking at their weakness and shortcomings, ought to seek to find out Christ in them. If we do so, we shall find how dear they will become to our hearts, and we shall love them. The natural tendency is, to look at the weakness and failings of others; but let us strive to overcome this, and, like the Lord Jesus Christ, see the beauty and comeliness of our Master in our fellow disciples.

CHRIST'S ESTIMATE OF HIS BRIDE

These are the particular lessons, which we have gathered from these verses—that Jesus sees beauty in us

His people, that He sees loveliness, that He sees the beautiful fruits and spices, to which reference is here made, which, although we do not find them in our gardens in this country, yet are they most precious fruits in the gardens of the East: and if He sees all this comeliness in us, surely we should see beauty and something to delight us in one another.

Now, further, in the description of the Church we read —"A fountain of gardens, a well of living waters, and streams from Lebanon." "A fountain of gardens." This does not mean a fountain producing gardens, as it might here be taken to mean, but a fountain in the midst of gardens. A fountain, the waters of which refresh and nourish the gardens. This He says further of His Church, and here He again uses three figures, even as we notice with regard to the first point. The figures are—first, "a fountain of gardens;" second, "a well of living waters;" and lastly, "streams from Lebanon."

"What do these figures imply? First of all, let us consider the figure—

"A FOUNTAIN OF GARDENS."

He means here, that in this world we are, or ought to be, for the refreshment and nourishment of one another; for the strengthening and invigorating of one another. Just as by a fountain in the midst of a garden, the plants are watered and nourished, and all the vegetation is benefited thereby, and the beautiful and fragrant flowers are refreshed: so the Church of Christ is left upon the earth to be a like blessing; not that she should merely enjoy His fullness herself, but in order that she should be for the fertilizing of those surrounding her, and especially that she may lend a helping hand to the brethren and sisters, particularly the younger brethren and sisters in Christ. This is the very purpose for which we are left in this world, that we may be as fountains of water, and especially for the strengthening and encouraging of one another, and the refreshing, nourishing, and watering of one another, even as the fountain in the midst of gardens.

But now, the second figure:

"A WELL OF LIVING WATERS."

What does this mean? In John 7:38, Jesus said, "He that believeth on me, as the Scripture hath said, out of his belly shall flow rivers of living water. But this spake He of the Spirit, which they that believe on Him should receive; for the Holy Ghost was not yet given, because that Jesus was not yet glorified." It was of the Holy Ghost He spake.

Now the Holy Ghost has been given. The Church in her collective capacity has received the Holy Ghost, and every individual believer has received that gift; therefore we are expected to be wells of living waters. There is no reason why out of you and me individually, there should not flow rivers of living water. The living water which has been given us ought to flow out to others. Have we all considered this, that for this very reason has been given to us the Holy Ghost? Just in order that we may minister to the world around us. We ought to be the means of good to our fellow sinners, and out of us there should flow rivers of living water, that poor sinners all around, young and old, rich and poor, whether enemies or friends, should be benefited.

And not merely so, but we should also be as wells of living water to the dear fellow believers. They oft may and do stand in need of refreshing and comforting, and it should be our aim to seek to be the messengers of this blessed help to these our brethren; we ought to aim so to live and act, that here, there, and everywhere, as God gives us opportunity, we may seek to spread far and wide the truth as it is in Christ Jesus. That is what is meant here—that we should not only be as fountains in the midst of gardens, but even as wells of living waters going out to benefit others; that out of us should flow rivers of living water.

Further, regarding this point, there is another figure used by the Holy Ghost—

"STREAMS FROM LEBANON."

"What is meant here? It goes still further than the other figures. When the snow melted under the summer sun on the heights of Lebanon, then mighty torrents poured down from the mountain, sweeping everything before them. Nothing could stand in the way of these streams. So should streams of living water flow out of us, with so much divine force and power, that the people of this world shall not be able to stand before us, but shall be constrained to say that of a truth God is with us.

If such were our state, we should carry away all before us, being strong in the Lord; and hundreds, yea thousands, would be converted. The whole Church surrounding us, which may be cold and dead, would be quickened and sot on fire, and all would be stirred up to new love and joy. Thus must we become blessings to many around us. Surely we ought all to aim after this, to be like "streams (torrents) from Lebanon."

We may have been idle, but let slumber and sleep rest upon us no more; and even when we have been stirred to some effort, let us not go back into a cold, lifeless state, but having done all to stand. "Stand therefore, having your loins girt about with truth; and having on the breastplate of righteousness, and your feet shod with the preparation of the gospel of peace; above all, taking the shield of faith, wherewith ye shall be able to quench all the fiery darts of the wicked. And take the helmet of salvation, and the sword of the Spirit, which is the Word of God; praying always and with all prayer and supplication in the Spirit, and watching thereunto with all perseverance and supplication for all saints."

That is to be our attitude—

STRONG IN THE ARMOUR OF GOD;

or, according to the figure which we have been considering, like mighty torrents coming down from Lebanon, carrying everything before them, and being never discouraged by anything we may meet. Because those mighty torrents, to which this figure likens us, were never discouraged or beaten back, but carried everything before them.

Oh, that this were impressed upon our hearts, that we have power as the disciples of the Lord Jesus Christ, and that we can accomplish great things by prayer and by faith; that none can withstand us, if we go in His power; that great as may be our enemies, yet greater is He that is for us than all that can be against us! And all the powers of darkness cannot withstand us, if we work in the strength of God and look to Him and trust in Him alone. For all that is before us cannot be accomplished by our own power or resources. If this were more deeply impressed upon our hearts, we should become more and more useful to the praise and honour and glory of God.

RECIPROCAL DELIGHT

But I must hasten on, as I have still two verses to speak of. In the sixteenth verse, to which we now come, the Church is speaking. The Lord Jesus Christ has spoken in the highest terms of the Church, and now the Church, His bride, speaks of Him in return. She delights in giving joy to the heart of the Lord Jesus; to see Him partaking of her fruit with pleasure, and to see Him gratifying His loving heart with her. Therefore she now says, "Awake, O north wind; and come thou south; blow upon my garden, that the spices thereof may flow out." Meaning, in other words, What I am I am for the Lord's sake. What I have received I have received for the Lord's sake. All that I have belongs not to me but to the Master, who has bought me with His precious blood. Therefore I take delight, joy, and pleasure in gratifying His Heart who bought me. All I have and all I am I take delight in rendering back to Him again.

It is with this feeling that the Church responds to the loving words of the Lord Jesus, "Awake, O north wind; and come, thou south; blow upon my garden, that the spices thereof may flow out," because the wind causes the spices and sweet fragrance of a garden to flow forth, so that the owner may enjoy the smell thereof.

And here we observe that whether it be the pleasant south wind or the strong, rough north wind, it is all the same; only that my blessed owner may be gratified by spices which flow out. Whether it be the sweet soothing influence of love, or the blows of affliction, it matters not, so that He is gratified by the display of the graces which He hath given.

But she proceeds to say: "Let my Beloved come into His garden, and eat His pleasant fruits." Do you seek thus to

GRATIFY THE HEART OF JESUS?

My beloved brethren and sisters in Christ, we can verily do so. Really and truly, poor, miserable sinners in ourselves though we are, we can gratify the heart of the Lord Jesus Christ. He is not personally here now,—He is gone up into Heaven. "We have to do with a risen Lord Jesus Christ, who is now at the right hand of God. Yet we can gratify the heart of this Jesus. We can cause sweet spices to ascend to Him; He can come into our company, even now, and enjoy our graces.

Shall I mention one of the ways in which, amongst many others, that might be mentioned, and which you must know yourselves, we can thus gratify His loving heart. It is this—"Inasmuch as ye have done it unto one of the least of these My brethren, ye have done it unto Me." There is a poor brother or sister without food, without clothes;

needing money, words of comfort or encouragement, or in any way a helping hand. Now, whatsoever ye do to that brother is done to and accepted by Jesus Christ as done to Himself.

Thus we shall gratify His heart in doing so. And we shall be saying, "Let my beloved come into His garden and eat His pleasant fruits." Let me ask you affectionately—are you doing this? Are you lending a helping hand to any weak or suffering brother, and in so doing gratifying the heart of the Lord Jesus Christ?

THE LORD'S RESPONSE

Now Jesus responds to the words of His bride—"I am come into My garden, My sister, My spouse; I have gathered My myrrh with My spices; I have eaten My honeycomb with My honey; I have drank My wine with My milk; eat, O friends; drink, yea, drink abundantly, O beloved." "What is this? I belong to Jesus, I am His sister, His spouse. I belong to the Church, that Church is His — by the grace of God we are what we are, by the grace of God we have what we have; all we have and are is His by divine right. While He accepts the longings of our heart to offer ourselves to Him, still He would have us remember that we do belong to Him.

Thus the Lord Jesus Christ brings before us, that we are His and have received all we have from Him. He would have us keep in mind that we are His through Him, and what we have is through Him. "We are wholly His, and to the very last day of our earthly pilgrimage, all we ever have in the world is of Him. While therefore the Church invites Him to come into the garden and partake of the pleasant fruits, yet He claims it as His own by right. He does accept and rejoice in our offer of it, but would have us understand that it is already all His own.

THE INVITATION

Lastly, "Eat, O friends; drink, yea, drink abundantly, O

beloved." If there be anyone who desires to partake of these blessings, the Lord Jesus Christ says to him, "Eat, O friends; drink, yea, drink abundantly." "Which literally means, "be drunk with love." Oh, aim above everything after this—to increase and abound in love; as it were, to be drunk with love—intoxicated with love! Oh, that we might know something more of this, and be so brimful of love to Jesus, and brimful of love to everyone, that it were running over to all around us! Jesus delights in seeing us filled with love, intoxicated with love, drunk with love. May we aim increasingly after this!

THE POWER OF THE KING

The subject for our consideration, beloved Christian friends, is "The Power of the King." This subject is full of comfort for each one of us. All the children of God, while yet in the body, are most weak in themselves, though we can do all things, through Christ who strengthens us, by exercising faith in Him day by day, hour by hour, moment by moment, seeking to lay hold on His strength, that we may have power. In ourselves we are most weak, by reason of the old corrupt nature remaining in us, and we shall remain *in ourselves* most weak, to the end of our course; therefore this subject is full of comfort, full of instruction, full of exhortation, full of warning, too, in a certain sense. But the great point, in the first place, is that we are

ONE WITH THE KING

There is no blessing to be had from the King, unless we are reconciled to God by faith in the Lord Jesus Christ. Naturally we are alienated from God; naturally we are "dead in trespasses and sins;" naturally we are afraid of God, on account of a guilty conscience. There is therefore no such thing as drawing strength out of God, nor is there a *possibility* of drawing strength out of Him, until we are made alive spiritually, until we are regenerated. And how are we to be regenerated? By believing the Gospel; by faith in the atoning death of the Lord Jesus Christ. Therefore, should there be any here present (as peradventure there are), who are as yet not reconciled to God by faith in the Lord Jesus Christ, who have still a guilty conscience, who are still unforgiven—let me beseech and entreat such, with all earnestness to care about their souls, and no longer to go on without obeying the Gospel. Remember that we are commanded to obey the Gospel—that it does not rest with us whether we like it or do not like it, we are commanded to obey the Gospel; beloved, we are commanded to believe in the Lord Jesus Christ. The great sin of man in his natural state is, that he does not believe the Gospel. Should there be any here present who do not see that they are sinners, let me beseech them with all earnestness to read the first three chapters of the Epistle to the Romans; and if they do desire to find out that they are sinners, God the Holy Ghost will show to them through that epistle most assuredly what they are by nature; and should any here present see that they are sinners, but have not yet believed in the Lord Jesus Christ for the salvation of their souls, yet desire to believe, if they could only just groan out a few words to God and say, "Have mercy upon me, O God, and help me to believe in the Lord Jesus Christ," God would help them to believe. It is through this faith in the Lord Jesus that we are regenerated. According to that Word, "Ye are *all* the children of God by faith in Christ Jesus," (Galatians 3:26) and according to that Word, "Whosoever believeth that Jesus is the Christ—is born of God," (I John 5:1), viz., that the poor despised, rejected Jesus of Nazareth is the promised Saviour, the Messiah; millions may say it, but none believe it except the children of God. Then, if we are regenerated we have life—spiritual life—and through faith in the Lord Jesus Christ we obtain the forgiveness of our sins, according to that Word in the 10th chapter of the acts of the Apostles, 43rd verse, where it is stated concerning the Lord Jesus. "To him give all the prophets witness, that through His name, whosoever believeth in Him shall receive remission of sins." Then, if we are regenerated—if we have obtained spiritual life, if the guilt is removed from our consciences, if we have become, through faith in Jesus, the children of God, then shall we enjoy the truth of "the power of the King." But should there be any one here present (I repeat it), who is as yet not a believer in the Lord

Jesus, then let me beseech and entreat him with earnestness to seek after forgiveness. Again, peradventure there are a few here who once enjoyed a cleansed conscience, who once walked in the ways of God, but who have now departed from Him. I desire that there may be none such present; but should this be the case, what have you to do? What you did at the first—to come as poor, miserable, guilty sinners, and confess your sins to God, exercising faith in the power of the blood of the Lord Jesus Christ, in which there is power to make you also clean again from your sins; the sins of back sliding will be forgiven and taken away by the power of the blood of Jesus Christ, just as the sins which were committed in our unregenerate state. Therefore see to it that you again obtain a cleansed conscience.—If there is power in the King, and we have a cleansed conscience (as by the grace of God I trust by far the greater part of us have), then oh, how precious to think that this

POWER IN THE KING IS TO HELP US IN OUR WEAKNESS.

The more we advance in the Divine life, and become acquainted with ourselves and with God, the more we see of the power of Satan and the corruptions within. The more we know of the temptations without, the more shall we be conscious day by day, and hour by hour, how weak we are in ourselves; and therefore we need the strong One to lean upon, to go to. That strong One we have in Jehovah Jesus. O the preciousness that we have not to do with a dead Christ! Though He was crucified and put into the grave on account of our numberless transgressions, yet He rose from the dead, He ascended up on high, and there at the right hand of God He is, for us who put our trust in Him, as the Living One, as the Mighty One, who takes delight and joy continually in helping us amidst all our weaknesses and frailties. When Paul stood alone, and every one of the brethren, by reason of the danger, had forsaken him, there was One who stood with him, there was One who was at his side. There was the King in power that blessed One never leaves us, never forsakes us. Let us rejoice in the knowledge of this.

I desire now to make a very few remarks (on account of the shortness of the time) on the various portions of Scripture which are brought before us as the subject for our consideration, The first is in Malachi 1:14: "I am a great King, saith the Lord of hosts."

REVERENCE

It is deeply important to remember that, while we are at peace with God, through faith in the Lord Jesus Christ, and while we are the children of God, and in fellowship with the Father and the Son, yet we are creatures and remain creatures, and therefore it becomes us to reverence God. On the one hand, they may not sufficiently walk in holy friendship with God I or, on the other hand, we may lose sight of the fact that we have to do with the Creator and Upholder of the universe, that He is a great King.

Let us not lose sight of this: for we must never forget that, while we are the children of God, and while we are partakers of the glory together with the Lord Jesus Christ, that yet we are creatures, and shall remain creatures, therefore it becomes us, as it were, to put off our shoes from our feet, and to consider that we are standing on holy ground. I affectionately press this on every one of my brethren and sisters in Christ; for the danger is lest we should lose sight of it, and in consequence make light of sin, by reason of our oneness with the Lord Jesus Christ.

POWER

The second point which is suggested to us is, "Where the word of a King is, there is power" (Eccles. 8:4). Most comforting and precious is this. For instance, with regard to all brethren and sisters in Christ who are engaged in service. "Where the word of the King is, there is power." What have we to do therefore? To pray for the word of the King, in order that there may be power; and therefore all who feel interested in the glory of God, and in the services of the Lord Jesus, should with earnestness seek, on behalf of all who are in anyway labouring for the Lord, His blessing, that the Lord the King would speak the word, and then the world would feel His power. The word, though uttered by mortal, sinful lips, if the King speaks through the instrument, will come in power. Let me affectionately beseech all who love the Lord Jesus in sincerity to see to it that with earnestness they help all who in any way seek the spread of the truth. Every one of us may exceedingly help all the beloved brethren and sisters who are occupied in this way. Then with all the efforts that are now made to spread the truth, let us especially keep before us this, that the Lord will be sought for blessing, and that, if there is little prayer, there will be little result; whilst the more abundant prayer there is brought before the Lord, the more abundant blessing we may reckon on. Therefore all of us with earnestness should see to it that the word of the King, which is the word in power, may come through the instruments who are seeking to spread the truth as it is in Jesus. But more than this, we have mighty enemies to fight against, and we have no strength of our own. We may say, "Get thee behind me, Satan," but the word of the King we need in our weakness—in our helplessness—the word of the King we need to subdue our natural evil tendencies—the word of the King we need in order that the world may not have power over us; and for this the King will be sought and entreated, and the more earnestly we give ourselves to prayer, the more we may expect to hear the word of the King, so that the world, the flesh, and the devil will be kept down, to the honour, praise, and glory of God, and the confounding of Satan.

The next point on which I wish to make a few remarks is, "The sceptre of Thy kingdom is a right sceptre" (Psalm 45:6). In

RIGHTEOUSNESS

the King rules, and this is what we have to keep before us. It is not only that in the world to come, when the Lord Jesus Christ has returned, there will be the rule in righteousness, but even now He rules in righteousness, and that is practically what we often lose sight of. There is given to us that precious word, "All things work together for good to them that love God;" but very frequently, when great trials and afflictions come—when we have to suffer from the world, when we are in weakness of body, when we have to sustain bereavements, losses, and the like—then the question arises, by reason of our old nature, why all this? And if we are not on our guard, we shall be inclined to entertain hard thoughts about God. But "the sceptre of His kingdom is a right sceptre;" "In righteousness He rules;" "Everything works together for good to them that love God." In joy or sorrow, however we may be situated, everything tends to our real good and profit, and it becomes us to be satisfied in our inmost souls (no matter how God deals with us) that all is for the glory of God, and for our real good and profit—all to make us increasingly to be conformed to the mind of God and to the Lord Jesus Christ; and therefore we ought to be satisfied with God's dealings with us in the darkest hours—we should kiss the hand that smites us. Oh, how we can glorify God under these circumstances, and show to an ungodly world the reality of the things of God! We can let them see that we do not differ from them in the matter of creed only, but that we are really children of God—that we have a Father in heaven, that we have a Friend in heaven, that we do not profess simply to believe the Word of God, but that we verily *do* so—that we *receive* the statement that "all things work together for good to them that love God." How could it be otherwise, but that all things work together for good to them that love God, since God gave the choicest gift He had to give in His only-begotten Son, and also promised that with Him He would freely give us all things? Therefore it becomes the children of God to be still, to be quiet, to know that God is dealing with them in everything, and to know that "all things work together for good to them that love God." Whether we see it, or whether we do not see it, His dealings are already working for our good. We have to exercise faith in this, and to be satisfied with the statement; that the sceptre of the King is a right sceptre; that everything He doeth is in righteousness; everything He doeth is good and like Himself.

The next statement is, that "a King that sitteth on the throne of

JUDGMENT

scattereth away all evil with His eyes." (Prov. 20:8). That Satan shall be bruised under our feet is the blessed, prospect before us—when by the power of the King he will have been bruised under our feet, when by the power of the King we shall have been completely delivered from everything contrary to the mind of God, so that when the will of God shall be presented to us, instantaneously in our inmost souls, we shall respond to the carrying out of His will. This time as not yet come, nevertheless we have in joyful anticipation to look forward to that day; and the more we can exercise faith with regard to the things to come—the realities of the heavenly day, the great day of the Lord Jesus Christ—the more shall we bring down the joys of heaven now into our souls already, the more spiritual power we shall have now: for, though we cannot have the office of apostles, we cannot say to what an extent we may, while yet in the body, overcome all the natural evil tendencies within us. The more we exercise faith in the power of the Lord Jesus, the more we practically use the power of the Lord Jesus Christ. If we make confession of our manifold failings and shortcomings, we may expect help to overcome what is contrary to the mind of God. There is also connected with the subject particularly this joyful prospect: the little flock is mixed up with the world. At present we are not separated from all them that hate the Lord; but this will be the case in that day when the whole heavenly family will be united, and in separation from those who do not love the Lord Jesus Christ. Are there any here present who will be separated, then, from us? Shall we all meet again as we meet under this one roof now? None, none will meet with the people of God, but those who trust in the atoning death of the Lord Jesus Christ. None, none will be found there in the glory, but those who were regenerated, before they were taken out of the world, through faith in the Lord Jesus Christ. O be in earnestness about this, if any be here present who are not yet believers in the Lord Jesus! for the power of the King will see to it, that none who are defiled enter the New Jerusalem. O the separation—the awful separation which will take place, it may be between parents and children, between brothers and sisters, between husbands, and wives! O see to it that none be separated from the people of God, in that day! We can only meet again in one place, if we are all believers in the Lord Jesus Christ; only then can we hear the word of the King, "Come, ye blessed of My Father, inherit the kingdom prepared for you from the foundation of the world."

THE CERTAINTY OF CHRIST'S TRIUMPH

A few words on the last passage: "He *must* reign till He hath put all enemies under his feet." (I Cor. 15:25). He *must* reign! O the comfort of this word, He *must* reign! Who will oppose the King of kings, the Lord of lords, the Almighty God the Creator of the universe, the Upholder of the universe? Who will withstand Him— Who will keep Him from reigning? O the joy we have in this—Jesus *must* reign! And it is particularly comforting in these days, when we see infidelity and Popery spreading, and all kinds and forms of superstition and error. How comforting to know that the truth must prevail! Jesus will triumph at the last. "He *must* reign." Every knee must bow before Him, every tongue must confess that Pie is Lord, to the glory of the Father. Bright and blessed prospect that thus it must be, that even those who now blasphemously speak against the Lord Jesus Christ will have to feel the power of the King, they will have to see that the King has power. He will triumph at the last. And now we who are united to the King, we who are of the little flock, most weak and helpless in ourselves, yet because we are united to the King who must reign—to the King who will triumph over every enemy—therefore we also, however weak and helpless in ourselves, through Jesus our Lord shall eminently triumph. That is the bright and blessed prospect before us! I am a poor sinner, and nothing at all, let us say to ourselves, but my Lord Jesus will help me, my Lord Jesus will obtain the victory for me; let me only cling and cleave to Him, let me only look to Him, let me day by day seek to exercise faith in His power, and all will be well at the last. We shall have the victory over Satan, over the evil spirits, over everything that opposes itself to our blessed Lord.

THE KNOWLEDGE OF CHRIST
"That I may know Him."—Phil. 3:10

It appears to me, beloved Christian friends, that with regard to the subject before us, "That I may know Him," the Holy Ghost, speaking by the Apostle, has no particular reference to the measure of knowledge which is absolutely needful with regard to the salvation of our souls, but a higher, further, more intimate acquaintance with the Lord Jesus Christ, even as a friend is intimately acquainted with his bosom friend. That this is the meaning, I gather from reading verse 8th in connection with verse 10th: "Yea, doubtless, and I count all things *but* loss for the excellency of the knowledge of Christ Jesus my Lord." Then what follows up to our portion before us, I judge to be a parenthesis, so that the connection would be—"I count all things but loss for the excellency of the knowledge of Christ Jesus our Lord, that I may know Him, and the power of His resurrection, and the fellowship of His sufferings," the parenthesis commencing from these words in the 8th verse: "For whom I have suffered the loss of all things and do count them but dung, that I may win Christ, and be found in Him, not having my own righteousness which is of the law, but that which is through the faith of Christ, the righteousness which is of God by faith." This parenthesis, it appears to me, refers to that which he has attained to already as a believer in the Lord Jesus Christ, and to which multitudes of the dear children of God have attained, but with which they should not be satisfied, but aim after greater attainments than these, even that they should know Him, and the power of His resurrection, and the fellowship of His sufferings.

The question arises naturally, What is it that the Apostle particularly desires in our text, "That I may know Him?" That be might know the Blessed One in all His loveliness, in all His beauty, just as the saints finally will see the King in His beauty, will know Him in all His loveliness, in all His characters, so as every one of His saints will know Him in the glory finally, so, while, the Apostle was yet in the body, whilst yet in weakness, whilst yet Satan was not bound, and himself not in the glory, he desired more and more intimately to become acquainted with the precious adorable Lord Jesus Christ in all His loveliness, so that the joy and the blessedness of the glory in the world to come might, in a great measure, already be realized by him while he was yet in the body.

PRACTICAL RESULTS OF KNOWING CHRIST

What would be the result of this intimate knowledge of the adorable Lord to which the Apostle refers here? Evidently it would be increased conformity to the image of our Lord Jesus Christ, according to the word of the Apostle John: "Beloved, now are we the sons of God; and it doth not yet appear what we shall be: but we know that, when He shall appear, we shall be like Him; for we shall see Him as He is," (or know Him as He is). So knowing the Lord Jesus Christ perfectly, knowing Him in all His loveliness, seeing the King in His beauty, they will be made like Him. Now in the measure in which we, the children of God, while yet we are upon earth, know the Lord in all His beauty, in all His loveliness, in all His characters, we shall be conformed to the mind of the Lord Jesus Christ. And on this account, this knowledge here referred to by the Holy Ghost, through the Apostle, is of such immense value. And we should not say, "I know him for the salvation of my soul. I shall at last be saved through Him." God be praised if we know the Lord sufficiently with regard to the salvation of our soul; but this is not the ultimate object regarding us, but the glory of His name, and our increasing conformity to the mind of the Lord while yet here on earth; and in order to bring this about, increased intimate acquaintance with the precious Lord Jesus Christ is to be sought after, so that one ought not to be satisfied with the measure of attainment regarding the knowledge of Christ to which he has been brought already. This is the first point then to which I desire to direct your attention, namely, that, with increased knowledge of the Lord Jesus Christ, there would be found in us increased conformity to the mind of the Lord Jesus Christ.

Another point that would be attained is increased spiritual power, increased comfort, increased strength in every way. I refer you, as proof of this, to the 4th verse of the 50th of Isaiah. Isaiah, you know, speaks here about the Lord Jesus Christ. There the Blessed One Himself stated for the comfort and the encouragement of His Church, "The Lord God has given me the tongue of the learned, that I should know how to speak a word in season to him that is weary." Therefore, the great point is to be able to treat the Lord Jesus Christ as a bosom friend, to be able to go to Him and say "My precious Lord, speak to me the word in season," when we are weary. Whilst passing through this vale of tears, in the midst of trial and difficulty, in the midst of labour and sadness, in the midst of sore temptation, in the midst of conflict of greater or less degree, again, and again, and again, the child of God, who desires to walk in the ways of the Lord, will find himself spiritually worn. Now then go to the precious Lord and say, "My Lord, speak to me the word in season, for I am weary."

These happy conference meetings are not so much for theological discussion as for spiritual encouragement. I ask, therefore, my brethren and sisters in Christ, how much do you know of this? Are you in the habit of going to the Lord Jesus Christ and saying, "My Lord, speak to Thy servant the word in season, for I am weary." I tell you as one who has known the Lord Jesus fifty years and eight months; again and again, and again, have I thus come to the Lord and said, " Lord speak a word in season to thy servant who is weary." And what have I found? Invariably this—I bear the testimony to the honour of my precious Lord—invariably this, He hath spoken to me the word in season when I have been weary. And let my beloved brethren and sisters in Christ but try the way. Seek to prove the blessed Lord Jesus in this way, and they will find now ready that Blessed One is to speak to them the word in season when they are weary. These are not merely religious statements, but fit to be treasured up in our hearts and to be known experimentally. But if you find it thus, oh the blessedness of that state of heart to have a friend ready at all times and under all circumstances to speak to you the word in season when you are weary! Oh, the blessedness of this indescribable, and if any of my friends have not known this preciousness, let me entreat them not to give themselves rest till they know the Lord Jesus Christ as a bosom friend!

But this is not all. Another result that would follow is this. Thus becoming increasingly acquainted with the Lord Jesus Christ, we should finally get into the state to which we find reference made in Psalm 9, 10th verse: "They that know Thy name will put their trust in Thee." And therefore we say, knowing Him they confide in Him, they trust in His power, they trust in His love, they trust in His wisdom, they trust in Him at all times and under all circumstances. How blessed such a state of heart would be! The world without looks on and wants to know if our religion is more than a mere difference of creed between themselves and us, to know how much we have of the reality of the things of God. Now if they find a man or a woman able at all times, under all circumstances, because they have a bosom friend in heaven, Almighty and infinately wise, who loves them at all times, and under all circumstances, who will ever help

PRACTICAL RESULTS OF KNOWING CHRIST

and succour and bless them, and therefore they are able to confide in Him, to look to Him, to trust in Him, to be quiet to be calm, and at peace, whatever the circumstances, and to be able to say: "Though He slay me, yet will I trust in Him;" then can the world surrounding us look on and see the blessedness and the reality of the things of God? And on this account it is of such vast moment not to be satisfied with knowing enough of the Lord Jesus Christ for the salvation of the soul, but to seek intimately to become acquainted with; Him, to know Him as a friend knows His bosom friend, and thus wholly to trust in Him. This blessedness I may tell you I have found in all the varying conditions of life. Oh! try Him, try Him, try Him! You will find how well it is to confide in Him, and how well you may confide in Him, and He will help you and never leave you nor forsake you.

Another, and the last reason why all this is so deeply important that we should seek increasingly to become acquainted with the Lord Jesus is this. All of you, my beloved brethren and sisters in Christ, know that weave in fellowship with the Father, and with His Son Jesus Christ, that we are in co-participation with the Father, and with His Son Jesus Christ, that means in partnership with the Father, and with His Son Jesus Christ. Now does not every one see how deeply important it is to know who our partner is, to know the riches of the partner, to know the means of one's partner, to know the disposition of the partner, to know the ability of the partner, to seek increasingly to acquaint ourselves with Them regarding whom God in the riches of His grace declares that we are in fellowship, in co-participation, in partnership with, the Father and the Son? How wondrous the condescension of that Blessed One to vile, worthless, wretched beings like us. While yet in weakness and yet exposed to the powers of darkness, and a pilgrim here on earth passing through, this vale of tears, how important that I should be able to go without fear to

Him, the good and gracious, and ever generous partner, the Lord Jesus Christ, who is infinitely rich and wise, and who loves me with an eternal and unchangeable love.

HOW TO ATTAIN THE KNOWLEDGE OF CHRIST

But some may say, "All this is most precious, but how may I attain unto it?" Of course, in the first place, we must have passed sentence on ourselves, must have condemned ourselves, and put our trust in the Lord Jesus Christ for the salvation of our souls. Without this there can be no such thing as attaining to this more intimate knowledge of the Lord Jesus Christ. This is absolutely needful. But as I stated at the beginning, it appears to me there is referred to here a higher degree of acquaintance with the Lord Jesus Christ, more than that which is necessary for the salvation of our souls, in order that we may glorify God, live as becomes the children of God, and bear fruit abundantly, sixty-fold, and a hundred-fold. I just mention here, and have my beloved brethren and sisters in Christ ever thought of it, that we are not to be satisfied with bearing fruit thirty-fold, but actually forty-fold, forty-five-fold, fifty-fold; to press on; yea, if it might be, to attain to bearing sixty-five fold, and if any of us have attained to this, then to aim at attaining seventy-fold, seventy-fivefold, eighty-fold; yea, to be satisfied short of nothing than to aim at one-hundred-fold. When the blessed Lord Jesus Christ brings this statement before us, He means what He says, that some bear in one and some in another degree. And why should we not advance to bear the higher and more glorious degrees, till the glorious consummation of one-hundredfold? We should never lose sight of the fact that the salvation of our soul is not the ultimate object that God has, but the glory of His name is intimately connected with our bearing fruit. Let us not think, that because we have now for a few years in some little measure left the world that we may take our ease, and now go oh, more quietly, but to press on, to press on, to press on, and to set before us nothing short of the prize, the bear-a hundred-fold.

Let us take the test in its connection. How may I attain to this intimate knowledge of the Lord Jesus Christ? In the 8th verse we read, "And I count all things but loss for the excellency of the knowledge of Christ Jesus my Lord," "that I may know Him and the power of His resurrection and the fellowship of His sufferings." Everything he desired to put aside and renounce, in order that he might know Him, and that increasingly he might become acquainted with Him. Therefore, beloved friends, the pleasures of this world are to be put aside—the fashion of this world to be laid down at the feet of Jesus, the riches of this world, the honour of this world, and all that the natural mind craves after, desires, finds gratification in—all to be laid down at the feet of Jesus, in order that we may be able to say with the apostle, "Yea, doubtless, and I count all things but loss for the excellency of the knowledge of Christ Jesus." So that we have for the remainder of our life but one single object. Not six, not five, not three, not two, but one single object—to live for God.

TRANSFORMED IN MIND

The subject for our consideration this evening is "Being transformed by the renewing of our minds." The connection in which this stands, the dear Christian friends know: "Be ye not conformed to this world, but be ye transformed by the renewing of your mind." As the redeemed of the Lord, it becomes us continually to keep before us, that our own salvation is not the ultimate end, but the glory of God. This we have never to lose sight of; and in order that we may do our part as witnesses for God in this world, it is necessary that we should not be conformed to the world, but transformed. Without this it is entirely impossible to be witnesses for God in a right way. We may think we do this and we do another thing to the glory of God, and yet just only in so far as we are not conformed to this world, but are transformed, are we truly witnesses for God.

Now as we have been bought by the precious blood of the Lord Jesus Christ; as God in Christ has done so much; as that precious and adorable Lord Jesus Christ has done so much for us, it well, becomes us that we, the sons of the Most High, should not wait for the glory, in order *then* to aim at being conformed to the image of God's dear Son (though then it will be perfect conformity to that Blessed One), but as far as in us lies to aim at it day by day already in this world. Now then, the first thing that we have to keep before us is just this; that it is the will of the Lord that we should be transformed.

Another point for our comfort is that this is possible— that it can be done through the renewing of our minds. The latter we have to keep as much before us as the former.

NOT DOING OUR OWN WILL

First, then, it is the will of the Lord that we should be transformed. In our natural state we all go the way of the world—that is, we go our own way, We may be amiable people in the eyes of our fellow men, we may be honest and moral, and every one may speak well of us even before our conversion; but yet we go our own way, and in this state it is entirely impossible to please God, because we set Him not before us. We do not what we do to the praise of His name. We use our bodily strength, our mental powers, our talents and gifts, just as we please, in order to gratify ourselves. We do not use them to the praise and honour and glory of God. We do not use our profession, our business, our money for the Lord, but we use them just as it pleases us, because we go naturally our own way; and that is just how we dishonour the Lord, how all natural men, through their living to themselves and not living for God, do dishonour God, cannot but dishonour God, and until we are renewed by the Holy Ghost things will go on in this way. All the resolutions that we may make to be in a different state will not alter the case.

> "Day by day we go astray,
> Day by day we go our own way,
> As sheep astray."

That is just what dishonors God, because we set Him not before our eyes. We do not live for Him: our time is not given to Him. Why? Because the heart is not given to Him. Our talents are not given to Him, because the heart is not given to Him. We go our own way. We set Him not before us, and therefore we live to ourselves, we please ourselves; and thus it will go on, until we are convinced that we have been sinners needing a Saviour, and until, as poor, lost, ruined, guilty sinners, we have put our trust in the Lord Jesus Christ, and have accepted salvation through His atoning sacrifice alone. In this way we are by the power of the Holy Ghost renewed. In this way we obtain spiritual life, and then begins the possibility of being transformed. Before that, it is impossible to be transformed, because we are dead in trespasses and sins. We are without spiritual life. Before the Holy Ghost has been given to us, and has renewed us through the belief of the gospel, we have no power to please God and to live for God, but we shall go on, to a greater or less degree, only to be conformed to the world, and to live to ourselves. So, then, should any be present who, up to this time, have been conformed to the world, and who have, nevertheless, a longing to be transformed, then let me say to such, dear friends, the only way to he transformed is, by the reception of the gospel, by believing the gospel, so that, through faith in the Lord Jesus Christ, we are born again: for until we receive the gospel, until we believe in the Lord Jesus, Christ, every one is dead in trespasses and sins; every one lives to himself; more or less, every one is conformed to the world, and must be, and cannot possibly be transformed from the world. And, therefore, since the only way to be transformed is to receive the gospel, this is the first deeply-important point; for by this the foundation is laid, and only in this way the foundation can be laid.

But whilst thus the beginning is made, it is only the beginning, and we should not be content with the beginning; but our hearty desire should be this, that not only for a few months after we have received the gospel we may be in some little degree transformed, but that thus it be month after month, year after year, ten years one after the other (if life is prolonged, and the Lord Jesus tarrieth); so that persons who knew us ten, twenty, thirty, forty, or fifty years ago as disciples of the Lord Jesus Christ, and see us ten, twenty, thirty, forty, or fifty years after, still find us in just the same way. Now, in order that it may be thus; in order that we may show our love and gratitude to our heavenly Father by being witnesses for Him in this evil world, and not waiting till the time of glory comes, and satisfying ourselves with saying that "I shall one day be conformed to the image of God's dear Son," there must be

PROGRESS IN THE DIVINE LIFE.

In order that already in a goodly measure it may be the case in this life, I desire to throw out a few hints, by the attending to which and the blessing of God we may make progress in the Divine life, and become more and more conformed to the image of God's dear Son. We have not to forget that the eyes of the world are upon us, that they want to see whether there is a difference between us and themselves—whether our lives witness for God, or whether they do not. Now, in order that it may be so, that more and more we aim after conformity to the image of God's dear Son, and that already in this life, in some measure at least, we make progress in this conformity to the image of God's dear Son, it appears to me, in the first place, a matter of deep moment, that day by day we seek to keep before us what we have been redeemed from, and what we have been redeemed unto. Just in the measure in which it is kept before our minds that once we belonged to the power of darkness, that once we were the slaves of the wicked one, that once we were the children of the devil, and that we have been brought out of this state, that we have been transplanted into the kingdom of God's dear Son, and that we are no longer dead in trespasses and in sins, as once was the case, and that we are no longer the slaves of the world and our own wicked, evil hearts—so shall we he constrained by love and gratitude to aim at this, that we shall seek increasingly to be conformed to the image of God's dear Son.

WHAT WE ARE SAVED UNTO

And, then, not only to keep before us what we have been redeemed from, but what we have been redeemed unto. All our sins forgiven—already, now; justified before

God through faith in the Lord Jesus Christ; begotten again, children of God for time and eternity, and as such, the heirs of God and the joint-heirs with the Lord Jesus Christ, ere long we shall reign with Jesus, ere long we shall sit with Him on the throne, and with Him judge the world—yea, Satan even, and the fallen angels. I say the more this is kept before us, that we shall spend a happy eternity in glory, together with the Lord Jesus Christ, that our own eyes shall see that blessed One, that our own hands shall be allowed to touch that blessed One, and that, in seeing Him as He is, we shall be like Him, not only obtaining the glorified body, but be perfectly free for ever and ever from every sin—the more this is kept before us, the more shall we be constrained in this world already to seek the glory of God.

Further, we have to aim at this, that we keep it before us, that it is the will of the Lord that the human creature should not be happy while walking in separation from God. It seems to me a matter of deep moment that this should be a settled conviction in our minds, that what God has determined is, that the human creature shall be wretched and miserable going his own way, and that peace and joy in God and in the Holy Ghost can only be obtained by walking with God—by walking in the fear of the Lord. Now if this were really the deep conviction of our hearts, a settled thing in our hearts day by day, as assuredly as I go my own way, as assuredly as I live to myself, so assuredly must I be wretched and miserable, because I walk in separation from God. Were this deeply impressed upon our hearts, we should aim after walking in the fear of the Lord.

LIVING TO PLEASE GOD

And, therefore, in the next place, it should be our deep, hearty longing, to have but one single object for our life—to live for God, to please God, since it is impossible that, in going our own way, we should be happy, we could really have peace and joy in the Holy Ghost. Therefore, to have this settled purpose of heart, that for the rest of the days of our life we will live for God, and for God only, and thus to dedicate the whole heart to God—not a part of it, but the whole of it—that is what is wanted. And this is a matter of the deepest moment, my beloved brethren and sisters in Christ; and should there be anyone amongst us with whom it is a question whether half the heart or three-fourths of the heart are given to the Lord, or whether the whole heart has been given to the Lord, then let me beseech such, my beloved brethren in Christ, not to be satisfied, till they come to this, that the whole heart is given to the Lord, so that we can stand before the Lord and say, "My Father, Thou knowest all things; Thou knowest that Thy poor child is feeble and weak, but Thou knowest also that my heart is given to Thee: Thou hast my heart." Thus it should be with us; and if it is not thus, oh! let us be determined not to leave this Conference Hall without coming to the purpose that the whole heart shall be given to the Lord.

But, then, my beloved brethren, we have not to lose sight of this, that though the whole heart is given to the Lord, and we desire with our whole heart to live for the Lord, that in ourselves we are weak and feeble. We have no strength of our own, and we must adopt certain means whereby, with the blessing of God, we shall be kept in this frame of heart, and shall go on in this frame of heart—not merely to have it for an hour or two, or a day, or a week, or a month, but to have it for all the remaining days of our life.

Now in order that it may be thus, it is a matter of the greatest moment that we remain conscious of our own weakness, and nothingness, and ignorance, all the days of our lives; and, therefore, in simplicity, in the consciousness of our weakness, and feebleness, and nothingness, cling and cleave to our heavenly Father in prayer. We must be men and women given to prayer; day by day going to our heavenly Father for help, strength, support, wisdom, for everything that we need, thus speaking to our heavenly Father. But, then, coupled with this must be, letting Him speak to us. When we pray, we speak to Him; and when we read the Word of God, our heavenly Father speaks to us.

LOVING THE WORD OF GOD

Here I again ask my beloved Christian friends: Are we really men and women who love the Word of God? How does it stand with us in this matter? Now since our happy Conference meetings last June how has it been with us? How much have we been reading of the Word of God? Have we once been reading through the whole of the Bible? Oh! beloved in Christ, it is a matter of deep moment that we are men and women given to the reading of the Word of God—regularly reading it, consecutively reading it; but, then, we should couple with this—meditation. Meditate, if it only be for a short time, upon only a small portion of the Word, and do this always with reference to our own hearts. Always meditate with reference to our own hearts, and read the Word of God practically, as the Word of God, so that our fallen reason bows before it. It is God who says it, and that should be enough for us, whether we can understand it with our fallen reason or not. "What thou knowest not now thou shalt know hereafter" is applicable in this respect also, and we should patiently, and prayerfully, and believingly wait till that time comes when we shall see why it is so, and why it is expressed in this way and not in another. But always have it before us practically, that the Holy Scriptures contain the Word of God, and therefore it becomes the fallen human being to bow before the Word of God.

But we should mix with the Word faith, and we should read and ponder it with the especial object of carrying it out in our life. If this is neglected, prayer will profit us very little; and the reading of the Word will profit us very little, if we do not mean to act according to it. It is given to us for the very purpose that we should act according to it; and in doing so comes blessing to the soul. In doing so our peace and joy in the Holy Ghost will he increased more and more. The blessedness of this I have known in my own happy experience for the last forty-seven years and nine months, and I can recommend this very particularly to my beloved younger brethren and sisters in Christ. Let us be honest. Let us never cease to act according to the Scriptures, and then with whatever weakness (at the first this may be the case) we shall surely make progress, we shall get further and further in knowledge and in grace.

CONFESSION OF FAILURE

Now if any one after all this fail in any way, what then? Simply honest confession at once, without hypocrisy or without seeking to excuse our failure. There should be unmistakable confession before our heavenly Father, and then to seek to experience the power of the blood of the Lord Jesus Christ afresh with regard to our own hearts, and to lay hold on the promise: "If we confess our sins, He is faithful and just to forgive us our sins, and to cleanse us from all unrighteousness;" and to lay hold of that Word afresh, that the blood of Jesus Christ makes clean from all sin. And this being the case, afresh to consecrate the heart to God, afresh to yield ourselves to Him, and seek His grace with regard to the future.

Now if any one were to go on in this way, what would be the result? The fulfilment of the promise of our adorable Lord, "Whosoever hath, to him shall be given, and he shall have more abundance." As assuredly as any one walks in this way, he will be less and less conformed to the world, and more and more transformed. He will be more and more like Jesus. Though it be but little in comparison with what it may be, and what it ought to be, still there will be more and more conformity to the image of our precious, adorable

Lord even in this life. And He is worthy, that blessed One who laid down His life for us, who shed the last drop of His blood —He is worthy that we should seek to live for Him.

Oh, my beloved Christian friends, let us aim at this! You see we are come here in order to be strengthened with might by the Spirit in our inner man. We come here, not to be amused, not to have some things brought before our minds, and, after all, just to remain in the state in which we were before; but we are here, beloved Christian friends, in order that each one of us may obtain spiritual strength through these happy meetings. The Lord delights in giving us blessing; it is the very joy of His heart to give us blessing; and if we are only willing to receive blessing, He is sure to he ready to give, and to give far more abundantly than we ever expect to receive. It is a blessed thing, even for this life, to walk in the ways of the Lord; but what He looks to you for is the whole heart.

WHOLLY THE LORD'S

In this one thing we must be honest, that there does not remain to ourselves a part of the heart; He will have the whole heart. He says, "My son, give Me thine heart," not "part of thine heart." Nor does He say, "My son, give me a little of thy money;" but He says "Give me thine heart," and He will accept nothing in the room of the heart. When the heart is really given to the Lord, then the purse is given to Him also; then the profession and business are given to Him also; then our houses and lands belong to Him also; and all we have and are belongs to the Lord. At this we should aim, and with nothing short of it should we be satisfied.

Epitaph on the tombstone of Mr. Müller:
In Loving Memory of
George Müller,
Founder of the Ashley Down Orphanage
Born September 27th, 1805,
Fell asleep March 10th, 1898.

He trusted in God with whom
"nothing shall be impossible,"
and in His beloved Son Jesus Christ our Lord
who said "I go unto My Father,
and whatsoever ye shall ask in My name
that will I do that the Father,
may be glorified in the Son."
And in His inspired word which declares that

"All things are possible to Him that believeth."
And God fulfilled these declarations in
the experience of His servant by enabling
him to provide and care for about
ten thousand orphans.

———————

This memorial was erected by the
spontaneous and loving gifts
of many of these orphans.

Printed in the USA
CPSIA information can be obtained
at www.ICGtesting.com
LVHW010206130124
768848LV00004B/284